EDUCATION for RURAL PEOPLE

THE ROLE OF **EDUCATION,
TRAINING** AND
CAPACITY DEVELOPMENT IN
POVERTY REDUCTION AND
FOOD SECURITY

David Acker

Iowa State University
College of Agriculture and Life Sciences

Lavinia Gasperini

Natural Resources Management and
Environment Department
Food and Agriculture Organization of
the United Nations
(FAO)

FOOD AND AGRICULTURE ORGANIZATION OF THE UNITED NATIONS (FAO) - 2009

ISBN 978-92-5-106237-1

Foreword

his publication was developed to assist policy-makers dealing with rural poverty, food insecurity and education challenges confronting rural people. It seeks to address the correlation between education, empowerment and food security, mainly through a number of "good practice" case studies from all over the world. It is about strengthening their capacity to achieve food security.

Education in all its forms has the potential to empower people, by increasing their self-confidence, their capacity to improve their livelihoods and their participation in wider processes of social and economic change. This book identifies different dimensions of education and training for rural people that have proven useful in developing peoples' capacity to enhance food security. It covers formal as well as non-formal education, literacy as well as skills training.

At the international level, these different dimensions of education and training for rural people are dealt with by a variety of stakeholders, including the UN agencies. This publication is the result of the review of a collaborative effort between FAO, UNESCO and about 350 partners aiming at contributing to the implementation of the World Food Summit Plan of Action and the Dakar Framework for Action on Education for All (EFA).

FAO and Italy have consistently supported efforts aimed at providing stronger linkages between food security and education issues. While the dramatic food crisis, exacerbated by the serious financial and economic crisis has given impulse to a renewed effort of the international community to reduce the impact of these events on poor people and to prevent future emergencies, we are more than convinced that education for rural people must be an essential part of this endeavour. Education for Rural People (ERP) is a worldwide call to action for educating all rural children, youth and adults. The great majority of the so-called "hard-to-reach children" are concentrated in rural areas. Giving them a wider access to education has been identified by the G8 as one of the crucial issues of development in the field of education. It responds not only to the basic need of reducing inequalities and creating equal opportunities for all, but also to the imperative of providing rural people with better tools, skills and capacity.

We hope that this publication may contribute to further focusing the efforts of the international community in this field and to highlight the task of tackling both simultaneously, namely food security and education, which deserve equal attention and priority.

Jacques Diouf,
Director-General
Food and Agriculture Organization of
the United Nations (FAO)

Franco Frattini,
Minister of Foreign Affairs,
Italy

Acknowledgements

This book could not have been prepared without the assistance of many individuals who contributed their time, energy and expertise. The authors would like to take this opportunity to acknowledge these contributions. Special thanks go to Reginald Seiders for his work in developing the case studies used throughout the book and to Ingemar Gustafson, Janice Albert, Vera Boerger, Renzo Rosso, Teresa Savanella, Pieter Van Lierop for their kind review and their comments to the manuscript.

Most importantly, the authors wish to thank the Direzione Generale per la Cooperazione allo Sviluppo (DGCS – Directorate General for Development Cooperation) of the Italian Ministry for Foreign Affairs for the financial support in publishing and disseminating this document.

The authors wish also to thank the FAO Electronic Publishing Policy and Support Branch (KCII) for the important collaboration, as well as Alessandro Spairani, Francesca Bertelli, Véronique Le Vavasseur Todini for their very capable assistance during the preparation of this document, Elena Mazza for final editing, Pietro Bartoleschi for design and lay-out, Arianna Guida (studio Bartoleschi) for desktop publishing assistance and Marzio Marzot for his photo archive and advice.

Table of Contents

Acronyms

ADB	African Development Bank
ACE	Community Education Association
ADEA	Association for the Development of Education in Africa
AdexFAR	Appui au développement de l'expertise en formation agricole et rurale (Support to the valuation development in agricultural and rural training)
AIDS	Acquired Immunodeficiency Syndrome
AKADEP	Akwa Ibom Agricultural Development Programme
AprenDes	Innovaciones en Descentralización y Escuelas Activas (Innovations in Decentralization and Active Schools)
BRAC	Bangladesh Rural Advancement Committee
BRIGHT	Burkinabé Response to Improve Girls Chances to Succeed
CCODER	Centre for Community Development and Research
CDC	Community Development Committee
CEC	Community Education Committee
CGIAR	Consultative Group on International Agricultural Research
COPE	Community-Owned Primary School
CSD	Commission on Sustainable Development
CSRL	Center for Sustainable Livelihoods
CSSP	Community School Support Programme
DFID	Department of International Development (UK)
DGCS	Direzione Generale per la Cooperazione allo Sviluppo (Directorate General for Development Cooperation)
ECLAC	Economic Commission for Latin America and the Caribbean
EDUCO	Educación con Participación de la Comunidad (Education with Community Participation)
EFA	Education for All
EMIS	Education Management Information System
EQUIP1	Educational Quality Improvement Program
ERP	Education for Rural People
ESCUP	Educational Support to Children of Underserved Populations
FAO	Food and Agriculture Organization of the United Nations
FFS	Farmers Field Schools
GDLN	Global Development Learning Network
GFAR	Global Forum on Agricultural Research
GTZ	German Agency for Technical Cooperation

HIV	Human Immunodeficiency Virus
IBDR	International Bank for Reconstruction and Development
ICRAF	World Agroforestry Centre
ICT	Information and Communication Technology
IFAD	International Fund for Agricultural Development
IFPRI	International Food Policy Research Institute
IICA	Inter-American Institute for Cooperation on Agriculture
IIEP	International Institute for Educational Planning
IWGE	International Working Group on Education
LTT	Local Task Teams
MAFRD	Ministry of Agriculture, Forestry and Rural Development
MDG	Millennium Development Goal
MEST	Ministry of Education, Science and Technology
NGO	Non-governmental Organization
OECD	Organisation for Economic Co-operation and Development
OSCE	Organization for Security and Co-operation in Europe
PRSP	Poverty Reduction Strategy Paper
RCDC	Regional Community Development Committee
SEMCIT	Sustainability, Education and the Management of Change in the Tropics
SFT	Strategy Formulation Team
SIDA	Swedish International Development Cooperation Agency
SIFE	Student in Free Enterprise
SOFI	The State of Food Insecurity in the World
TVET	Technical and Vocational Education Training
UN	United Nations
UN-DESA	United Nations Department of Economic and Social Affairs
UN-DPI	United Nations Department of Public Information
UNDP	United Nations Development Programme
UNESCO	United Nations Educational, Scientific and Cultural Organization
UNFPA	United Nations Population Fund
UNICEF	United Nations Children's Fund
UPE	Universal Primary Education
USA	United States of America
USAID	United States Agency for International Development
USDA	United States Department of Agriculture
VEDCO	Volunteer Efforts for Development Concerns
WFP	World Food Programme
WSSD	World Summit on Sustainable Development

Executive summary

Nearly one out of six people of the current inhabitants of the world is suffering from hunger and illiteracy and the majority of them are in Africa. Education for Rural People (ERP) is a policy approach aimed at contributing to the reduction of the 963 million food insecure people, the 776 million illiterate adults and the 75 million illiterate children within the Millennium Development Goals (MDGs) framework. Education, labour, land, livestock and infrastructure are the key assets enabling rural households to escape poverty, and ERP is one of the most powerful weapons against hunger. A 2007 report from the British Department for International Development (DFID) indicates that more than US$ 11 billions are needed annually for education if Africa is to have any hope of getting all children into primary school by 2015.

This book presents a synthesis of lessons learned since the launch in September 2002 of the ERP global partnership designed to contribute to the acceleration of progress towards the MDGs.

ERP is one of the Partnerships for Sustainable Development of the United Nations Commission for Sustainable Development. The partnership – launched during the World Summit on Sustainable Development (WSSD) - is a worldwide *call to action* to foster rural people's capability to be food secure, to manage natural resources in a sustainable way and to provide education for all rural children, youth and adults. The partnership aims at contributing to remove barriers that prevent poor people from using their capacity including barriers such as the urban-rural knowledge and education gap. ERP works through the identification of political, institutional, organizational and individual opportunities and constraints that poor people face in accessing education and training services at all levels of education in both formal and non-formal settings. ERP seeks to empower the rural poor to become fully integrated actors of the development process by promoting collaboration among the education, agriculture and rural development sectors to ensure education and skills training to all rural people. The strategy addresses

research, knowledge generation and sharing, advocacy, policy and capacity development, as well as normative and field work. ERP is also one of the nine flagships of the Education for All (EFA) programme led by the United Nations Educational, Scientific and Cultural Organization (UNESCO). The ERP partnership flagship operates under the leadership of the Food and Agriculture Organization (FAO) of the United Nations and in close collaboration with UNESCO.

The most important products of ERP to date have been the knowledge generated and disseminated, the innovations identified, and the lessons learned by ERP partners related to policy and practice in areas such as education quality and access, gender-responsive learning environments, parent and community engagement, and accommodation of non-traditional learners, to name just a few. These knowledge products formed the basis for national and regional capacity development meetings worldwide.

Education is essential to FAO, as indicated in its Constitution "... the Organization shall promote and, where appropriate, shall recommend national and international action with respect to: ... the improvement of education ... relating to nutrition, food and agriculture, and the spread of public knowledge of nutritional

and agricultural science and practice ..." (FAO, 1945, Article I, 2b), to achieve the following goals:

>> "raising levels of nutrition and standards of living ...;

>> ... bettering the condition of rural populations;

>> and ... ensuring humanity's freedom from hunger" (FAO, 1945, Preamble).

ERP employed a research-based policy approach involving both FAO and UNESCO in promoting multisectoral alliances between ministries of education and agriculture. ERP worked simultaneously at the policy and field levels with an emphasis on the policy work to ensure the highest impact in terms of cost-effectiveness.

Research was conducted to collect successful responses to challenges confronting policy-makers and government and civil society frontline practitioners working to provide effective education and training for rural people. This information, as well as ERP good practices and training materials, was published in the global repository of the knowledge base of ERP (http://www.fao.org/sd/erp/) and shared worldwide through electronic and print formats so that the public could benefit from the experiences of others working in this field. The following table summarizes some of the important challenges and responses identified.

CHALLENGES	RESPONSES
(1) **Access to education and training**	Positive discrimination policies and programmes for rural people including: >> education and training fee removal >> free access to learning materials >> school feeding programmes to improve attendance >> free school transport programmes >> expansion of the school network and training centre construction >> double-shift classes and after-hours adult education >> targeting the needs of specific rural groups >> satellite schools in remote areas for the youngest children and girls >> application of Information and Communication Technologies (ICT) as appropriate
(2) **Quality of education and training**	>> improved teacher training professional development >> creation of conditions for teachers retention in rural areas and reduction of rotation >> design of training materials to address rural life problems >> combining academic and life skills for greater relevance >> use of school gardens as living laboratory and integration in school curriculum >> provision of a safe and adequate learning environment >> farmer participation in curriculum planning and training events >> use of improved monitoring and evaluation tools
(3) **Decentralization and community involvement**	>> combining national and local curriculum planning >> community participation in curriculum development >> community-based approaches to increase community ownership >> education that is relevant to rural livelihoods and the community >> parent-teacher associations to improve school resources >> involvement of community also through school gardens >> community monitoring of quality and relevance
(4) **Gender responsive learning environments**	>> flexible training programmes to accommodate labour peaks >> well-supervised boarding facilities to safeguard women and girls >> school meals for all rural children >> take-home rations for girls as an incentive for families >> half-day farmer training for women with responsibilities at home
(5) **Organizational and institutional efficiency**	>> coordination among ministries of education and agriculture >> coordination among public providers of extension and education, non-governmental organizations (NGOs) and the private sector >> multi-stakeholder participatory planning of programmes to support ERP >> extension officers running adult basic education classes

(6)	**Accommodating non-traditional learners**	>> flexibility in the training and education calendar to accommodate weather, cropping patterns, nomadic movements >> providing education for out of school rural children, youth and adults (especially girls and women), retired child soldiers, refugees and displaced persons, people in inaccessible and remote areas, disabled persons, ethnic minorities, working children, the elderly, nomads and pastoral communities, people suffering from diseases, and others >> use of front-line extension staff to reach remote audiences, use of farmer-to-farmer training approaches, use of non-formal basic education approaches
(7)	**Redefining agricultural education**	>> revised curricula at technical and vocational agricultural education and training colleges for improved training of technicians >> improved training of trainers for agricultural education >> agricultural education that reflects the fact that both on-farm and off-farm competencies and skills are important to sustaining livelihoods of people in rural areas >> agricultural education that reflects changes in technology, global supply chains, market and health challenges, on-farm and off-farm employment, environmental changes, and enterprise development
(8)	**Skills training for rural people**	>> increased and improved formal and non-formal skills training for youth and adults >> training for school drop-outs >> diversifying competencies and skills to reduce vulnerability and foster resilience to address shocks >> providing literacy and numeracy training together with skills training >> training in both life skills and job skills
(9)	**Recruitment and retention of extension staff and school teachers**	>> recruitment of teachers and extension staff from rural areas >> bonuses and higher salaries as incentives for rural staff >> provision of subsidized housing >> posting newly qualified staff in pairs >> creating career progression options >> provision of land and training in agriculture >> profit sharing in school-based income-generating activities
(10)	**Effective pro-rural people-centred policies**	>> increased financing for ERP >> education and training data disaggregated for urban and rural people >> policies that recognize the diversity of needs of rural people >> policies that recognize agro-ecological and geographical circumstances as well as socio-economic and cultural differences of residents of rural areas

ERP CHALLENGES

Key conclusions and policy considerations
addressed in this book include
(see Conclusions for more details on this subject):

>> **Considerable progress has been made.** Six years of policy, advocacy and capacity development work has led to important international recognition of ERP's key role in achieving the MDGs and especially of its key role in poverty reduction, food security and sustainable natural resources management.

>> **Much work remains to be done.** Despite the important progress made towards all eight MDGs, according to the United Nations, "we are not on track to fulfil our commitments" (UN, 2008, p. 3).

>> **ERP is an essential foundation stone for achievement of the MDGs.** Better educated rural people have better employment prospects, better health, greater food security, less vulnerability to shocks, and better coping mechanisms in dealing with the forces of climate change, food crises, globalization and challenges to cultural traditions.

>> **ERP is a policy and programme priority.** National governments, international agencies, bilateral donors and NGOs need to increase their policy and programme emphasis on ERP. In particular, UNESCO and the World Bank, given their lead roles in EFA and the Fast Track Initiative can ensure ERP becomes an integral part of Poverty Reduction Strategy Papers (PRSPs) and EFA National Plans.

>> **Funding for ERP needs to be a national and international priority.** Major policy and resource allocation shifts will need to take place if significant progress is to be made in poverty reduction and EFA. ERP needs an increased share of public resource allocations and needs to be at the core of National Rural Development and EFA Plans.

>> **Effective management of ERP requires reliable data.** Improved statistics as well as Education Management Information Systems (EMIS) are needed. Pro-poor policies call for the disaggregation of education and literacy data into rural and urban populations in the UNESCO international statistics, the EFA Global Monitoring Report, as well as within national EMIS.

>> **Partnerships are essential to progress**. Partnerships among international organizations, governments, non-governmental organizations, community-based organizations, universities, the private sector, the media and others will continue to be an essential ingredient of a successful ERP initiative.

>> **Intersectoral cooperation at national level.** Coordination between ministries of agriculture and education is essential if rural people are to be effectively served. Each has assets and expertise critical to these efforts.

>> **Working as One UN.** Intersectoral cooperation at the international level is essential. As the lead agency for the ERP partnership, FAO will continue to advocate for stronger governmental commitments for a higher level of resources for ERP. UNESCO and the World Bank are uniquely suited for facilitating ERP implementation at the national level within their mandates to support the advancement of education and training and given their privileged dialogue with ministries of education. UNESCO's leadership and technical support to ERP at the country level during this next phase would need to be strengthened, and FAO is in a good position to contribute as a supporting entity to the work of UNESCO in the specific areas of FAO expertise.

>> **Redefining agricultural education.** Today, a broader view of the life skills necessary to thrive in rural areas has emerged. There is a need to broaden the agricultural education paradigm to embrace the concepts of sustainable rural development.

>> **Needs-based approach.** The "one size fits all" standardized education strategies are not effective in reaching rural people. Rural people have a variety of specialized needs that have to be addressed to expand access and improve quality of education and training for children, youth and adults.

>> **There are many options for assisting rural people to develop their capacity.** These options have been successfully implemented in various countries around the world. This book was designed to support capacity development initiatives such as the 2009 UNESCO World Conferences, and further activities, including ERP specific initiatives.

>> **Rural girls and women are the most vulnerable.** Rural girls and women suffer geographical and gender discrimination. Strategies to boost rural girls' participation in education and female literacy include removing cost barriers, strengthening rural schools as gender-sensitive centres of quality learning, developing gender-sensitive learning content and school environments.

>> **Rural youth are the future.** Youth of today are the leaders and the farmers of tomorrow. Rural youth represent the majority of the population in the majority of less developed countries and explicit focus on their needs and potential contributions to our common future is urgent.

>> **The future challenges for ERP** arise from the fact that the vast majority of those excluded from education live in rural areas. Therefore, education for rural people is vital, urgent and essential if the MDGs are to be met.

Preparing rural citizens to engage successfully in knowledge-based economies, to respond to market and climate changes, to develop their resilience to address a variety of shocks, and to weather food crises associated with global economic shifts are essential to their well-being. Preparing rural people to be active citizens contributing to foster peace and democracy and enjoying long, healthy and creative lives is central to the achievement of the MDGs.

INTRODUCTION

I n *The State of Food Insecurity in the World 2006* (SOFI), the FAO Director-General, Dr Jacques Diouf, stated that "the concentration of hunger in rural areas suggests that no sustained reduction in hunger is possible without special emphasis on agricultural and rural development" (FAO, 2006, p. 6). This was reiterated by Dr Diouf in *The State of Food Insecurity in the World 2008*, with the added urgency brought on by high food prices. In June 2008, FAO hosted the *High-Level Conference on World Food Security: the Challenges of Climate Change and Bioenergy*. Rising food prices were a central theme of this important gathering.

In designing responses to these challenges, rural people will play a crucial role. Education, training and capacity development to foster rural people capacity to deal with these changing circumstances will be critical ingredients for the success of the campaign to reduce food insecurity and related shocks for the most vulnerable populations. With demand for food expected to rise by approximately 50 percent by 2030, it is essential to move aggressively to improve education, training and capacity development so that a knowledge-based response can be mounted in the face of this significant challenge. "Public investment in infrastructure, agricultural research, education and extension is indispensable for promoting agricultural growth" (FAO, 2006, p. 29).

However, several existing conditions will make progress in this area exceedingly challenging.

>> "Some 70 percent of the poor in developing countries live in rural areas and depend on agriculture for their livelihoods ..." (FAO, 2006, p. 28).

>> "... the world is now estimated to have 963 million malnourished people" (Diouf, 2009).

>> In the world, some 75 million children of primary school age are not in school.

>> Over four out of five of these 75 million children live in rural areas (UNESCO, 2008).

>> An estimated 776 million adults – two thirds of whom are women – lack basic literacy skills (UNESCO, 2008) and the majority of them are rural.

Inequity pushes substantial segments of society into exclusion and, in doing so, gives rise to discrimination and handicaps of all kinds, allowing an enormous potential in terms of factors and forces for development to wither away (FAO, 2006).

The rural-urban education gap has been addressed and overcome by the Organisation for Economic Co-operation and Development (OECD) countries as a key constraint to overall development. Inequity in education is directly related to the overall Gini coefficient of inequality of income distribution. Overcoming the knowledge and education gap in developing countries is not only crucial to economic growth but also to global and national democracy, peace and social cohesion, and generally to sustainable development.

The purpose of this book is to present a synthesis of lessons learned since the launch of the ERP partnership in 2002, under the leadership of FAO, as part of the implementation process for the Millennium Development Goals and the goals of the World Summit for Sustainable Development. This book was developed to assist policy makers in dealing with rural poverty, food insecurity and education challenges confronting rural people. It is also designed to assist adult and youth education professionals, extension managers and academics interested in

changing strategies for an increasingly knowledge-based economy. Lastly, it is intended for use by members of the ERP partnership and other practitioners throughout the world.

This books draws on the contributions of ERP partners throughout the world. It also builds on two previous articles by the authors:

>> Acker, D.G. & Gasperini, L. 2008. Education for rural people: what have we learned. *Journal of International Agricultural and Extension Education,* 15(1) Spring.

>> Acker, D.G. & Gasperini, L. 2003. Launching a new flagship on education for rural people: an initiative agricultural and extension educators can get behind. *Journal of International Agricultural and Extension Education,* 10(3) Fall.

The book starts with the background and rationale for the ERP initiative and the relationship with the mission of FAO and other partners. This context-setting section is followed by the analysis of the challenges faced by rural people and some innovative responses that are already in place identified through research. The ERP partnership is described to provide the reader with a full understanding of the variety and number of actors involved in implementing ERP. The book ends with a chapter recommending priority actions for future policy and field work.

This book was prepared as a contribution to the 2009 G8 and the UNESCO World Conferences on Education, as well as for the ERP future capacity development initiatives.

ERP BACKGROUND and RATIONALE

THE PURPOSE OF ERP

unger and illiteracy strike approximately one billion of the world's current population of 6.5 billion people. Within the Millennium Development Goals (MDGs) framework, ERP is a policy approach that aims at contributing to reduce the 963 million food insecure people (Diouf, 2009), the 776 million illiterate adults and the 75 million illiterate children (UNESCO, 2008). The essential assets enabling rural households to escape poverty are education, labour, land, livestock and infrastructure (FAO, 2007b), and ERP is one of the most powerful interventions to overcome hunger (Burchi and De Muro, 2007).

ERP is a people-centred approach that bridges the efforts of the agriculture and education sectors in bringing about transformation of rural communities by developing the capacity of rural people to feed themselves, to overcome poverty, hunger and illiteracy, and to enjoy long, healthy and creative lives (UNDP, 1999). The ERP policy approach broadens the agriculture production focus of traditional rural development approaches to encompass all those who live and work in the rural space and not only people directly involved in agriculture.

The research foundations of the ERP policy were laid in the FAO and UNESCO publication *Education for rural development: towards new policy responses* (2003). Education and skills training are seen as preparing rural citizens to succeed in part-time and full-time on-farm and off-farm employment and providing them economic and social competencies, mobility and resilience needed to live in a space that includes both farming and other economic and social activities. What is clear is that providing ERP is a complex challenge given the heterogeneous nature of the main stakeholders, the number of people involved in the world, and the particular physical, cultural, and resource endowments of rural space.

A PARTNERSHIP

ERP is also a global partnership promoted to accelerate progress towards the MDGs. The partnership – launched in September 2002 during the World Summit on Sustainable Development (WSSD) - is a worldwide *call to action* for educating all rural children, youth and adults (Diouf, 2002; UN, 2002). The partnership aims to remove barriers that prevent poor people from using their capacity, including the urban-rural knowledge and education gap. ERP is a member of the Partnership for Sustainable Development of the United Nations Commission for Sustainable Development (CSD) launched jointly by FAO and UNESCO Directors-General.

ERP works through the identification of political, institutional, organizational and individual opportunities and constraints that poor people face in accessing education and training services at all levels of education, in both formal and non-formal settings. ERP seeks to empower the rural poor to become fully integrated actors of the development process by promoting collaboration among the education, agriculture and rural development sectors to ensure education and skills training for all rural people (http://www.fao.org/sd/erp/). The strategy addresses research, knowledge generation and sharing, advocacy, policy and capacity development, as well as normative and field work.

Developing countries often face challenges in effectively delivering basic education services in rural areas because of the lack of trained personnel as well as an incomplete knowledge of policy alternatives. Weak coordination in addressing education in rural areas between ministries of education and agriculture, and with civil society is also a common constraint. Both FAO and UNESCO have been aware of these gaps, hence the launching of the ERP as a multi-partner, intersectoral and interdisciplinary capacity development initiative. ERP bridges the Earth Summit (1992), the World Food Summit (2006 and 2002), the WSSD (1992) and the EFA (1990 and 2000) policies and programmes. It also builds on the MDGs holistic policy approach that addresses economic growth and international competitiveness of the agriculture sector as part of the sustainable development and poverty reduction strategies, and includes education, health and social (also gender) equity and sustainable environment as key endeavours.

ERP is also one of the nine EFA flagships. The EFA flagships are multi-partner initiatives that focus on specific EFA-related areas and problems requiring special attention to implement the EFA Dakar Framework for Action. The ERP flagship is implemented under FAO leadership in collaboration with UNESCO and more than 350 partners.

WHAT DO WE MEAN BY RURAL?

Rural people live in human settlements with small populations and in geographical spaces often dominated by farms, forests, water, coastal zones, mountains, and/or deserts (FAO/UNESCO-IIEP, 2005a).

"Most rural dwellers work in agriculture, often for low rates of compensation. They face high transaction costs and have little political clout. The government services to which they have access are generally inappropriate and of poor quality. Rural people are generally farmers, stockbreeders, fishermen and, in some cases, nomads" (FAO/UNESCO-IIEP, 2007b, p. 15).

Rural people also deal with transformation and marketing of land and forest products and services (FAO/UNESCO-IIEP, 2005a).

Rural people are an overlooked majority of the world's poor population because of the prevailing western and industrial models of development that give more priority to the urban industrial and services sectors as the engine of national economic development. This urban bias leads to disregard the critical role of rural people in determining food security (MDG 1 – Reduce extreme poverty and hunger) and environmental sustainability (MDG 7 – Ensure environmental sustainability). This bias also leads policy makers to overlook the fact that rural people constitute the majority of out of school children and illiterate adults, and therefore investments in ensuring universal primary education (UPE), adult literacy and life-long education should mainly be directed to rural populations.

Rural people cannot be assumed to be a homogenous group. "Rural is plural", meaning that there is a wide variation in the needs of different groups throughout the world. Research points out a large degree of heterogeneity both within and across countries in terms of access by rural households to essential assets and services, including

education (FAO, 2007b). A new rurality is affirming itself: here, agriculture continues to be a very important component but it is not the <u>only</u> component that needs to receive attention in an effort to develop a comprehensive rural society (FAO/UNESCO-IIEP, 2006c). The majority of rural poor are illiterate and are engaged in subsistence agriculture. As illiterates, they are excluded from the knowledge that would improve their capacity and productivity, increase their income and food security, connect them to the market from which they are largely marginalized and enhance their livelihoods and citizenship (Burchi and De Muro, 2007).

RURAL PEOPLE ARE STILL A (NEGLECTED) MAJORITY
IN LESS DEVELOPED REGIONS

While rural people are still the demographic majority in less developed regions of the world, they are a political minority and an often-neglected demographic majority. According to the United Nations, "during 2008, ... the proportion of the population living in urban areas will reach 50 percent ... in the less developed regions the 50 percent level will likely be reached around 2019" (UN-DESA, 2008, p. 2). These data indicate that while from an overall global demographic perspective urban people have now equalled the rural population, in less developed regions the percentage and the absolute number of rural people (estimated to reach 3 104 196 000 in 2010 and 3 107 486 000 in 2030) are such that this demographic group cannot be ignored. Between 2010 and 2030, the rural population will decrease worldwide less than sixty thousand units.

Moreover, in less developed regions despite the emphasis given to urbanization, the United Nations data indicate that, at least for the next ten years, if current trends are maintained, the majority of the population will continue to be rural and that the absolute numbers of rural people will not change drastically for the next 20 years. This means that urbanization trends cannot be an alibi for not addressing rural people's basic needs and rights, including education and training. This is even truer in Sub-Saharan Africa where, in 2002, 70.6 percent of the population was rural. The rural population of Sub-Saharan Africa will continue to be predominantly rural: in 2015, it will be 60.2 percent and in 2030, 54.8 percent (UN-DESA, 2008). Overall demographic trends indicate that specific policies, efforts and further investments are needed to promote the wealth of rural people including greater distribution of educational opportunities within nations and globally in the world. Poverty reduction and food security cannot improve rapidly unless rural citizens are targeted for development assistance, including education, training and capacity development. Often, rural people move to urban areas looking for better living conditions and, in some cases, end up in illegal settlements or worse living conditions than in rural areas. ERP contributes to enhancing rural people livelihoods wherever they might choose to live.

RURAL PEOPLE ARE THE MAJORITY OF THE WORLD'S POOR

The majority of the world's poor – about 75 percent – including food insecure, illiterate adults and out of school children, live in rural areas and suffer from inequitable access to food, schools, health care, roads, technology, institutional support and markets (World Bank, 2007b; World Bank, 2007c). Urban citizens represent 25 percent of global poor. Owing to the fact that rural people lack a strong political voice, they are often at a disadvantage because of urban biased policies that lead to inequitable resource distribution favouring urban over rural people, including access to markets, infrastructure, health care and education (FAO ERP home page; IFAD, 2001).

WHY FOCUS ON EDUCATION FOR RURAL PEOPLE?

Illiteracy is strongly correlated with hunger and mainly a rural phenomenon hindering rural development and the wealth of each nation, threatens productivity and health, and limits opportunities to improve livelihoods. The evidence of the contribution of education to economic growth, the return to investment in schooling and the effects of education on unemployment and income distribution has long since been providing the research base for advocating for greater investments in education and especially in basic education (World Bank, 1988).

Research focusing specifically on education and rural development indicates that increased access to relevant and quality basic educational services for rural people contributes directly and positively to improved productivity, food security and livelihoods (Moock, 1981; Burchi and De Muro, 2007). A review conducted for the World Bank examined 18 studies that measure the relationship in low-income countries between farmers' education and their agricultural efficiency (as measured by crop production). The review concluded that the level of education of farmers was related to the level of their farm productivity, with four years of education contributing, on average, an 8.7 percent productivity gain over those with no formal education. The review also found that the effect of education is even greater (13 percent increase in productivity) where complementary inputs, such as fertilizers, new seeds or farm machinery are available (UNICEF, 1992).

"Literacy and formal schooling are linked with reduced fertility rates, improved health and sanitation practices and an increased ability to access information and participate in various social and economic processes" (FAO/UNESCO-IIEP, 2002, p. 25). ERP African partners noted that "... success in realizing the potentials of African agriculture will depend largely on that crucial factor of education" (FAO/UNESCO-IIEP, 2006b, p. 27). They questioned whether rural farmers are prepared to participate in an increasingly knowledge-based economy and smallholders can "compete in local and international markets in an increasingly globalized world, and in markets with stringent consumer demands, food safety and health requirements" (FAO/UNESCO-IIEP, 2006b, p. 26).

Knowledge and capacity development not only serve to increase productivity but also build people's identity and enable them to participate fully in social and political life (SIDA, 2000). As globalization moves the world from technology-based to knowledge-based economies (K-Economies), education and training will become even more crucial. Access to quality education and training for all will be the yardstick that will differentiate and govern the gap between rich and poor (UNICEF, 1992).

According to the *EFA Global Monitoring Report 2009* (UNESCO, 2008), an estimated 776 million adults – or 16 percent of the world's adult population – lack basic literacy skills. About two thirds of them are women. Among the 75 million out of school children, over four out of five live in rural areas, mostly in South and West Asia and Sub-Saharan Africa. The majority of them are rural girls. In Africa, the challenge is greater than in other regions. A report from the British Department for International Development (2007) stated that more than US$ 11 billions are needed annually for education if Africa is to have any hope of getting all children into primary school by 2015. These rural illiterate children add every year to the number of illiterate adults, determining that the majority of illiterate adults are also rural people, and prevalently rural women. Given the two-sided relation between hunger and education, progress on MDG 1 and MDG 2 (Achieve universal primary education) are closely interconnected and ERP is crucial to achieving both. Progress in these areas is also vital to the achievement of other MDGs, especially those for which FAO and UNESCO have the lead role (MDGs 1 and 7 for FAO, MDG 2 for UNESCO).

LES FEUX DE BROUSSE ONT DES CONSEQUENCES NEFASTES SUR L'ENVIRONNEMENT C'EST LE CAS DE CET HOMME QUI A BRULÉ TOUT UN VILLAGE EN METTANT UN FEU DANS LA BROUSSE.

Ensuring access to and completion of quality education for this "neglected majority" of the world's poor living in rural areas is a major challenge to the achievement of the EFA targets. Specifically, the need to include rural people in the education system is crucial to ensuring that, by 2015, all children have access to free and compulsory primary education of good quality; achieving a 50 percent improvement in levels of adult literacy by 2015; and ensuring that the learning needs of all young people and adults are met through equitable access to appropriate learning and life skills programmes (UNESCO, 2000). The lack of learning opportunities is both a cause and an effect of rural poverty. Hence, education and training strategies for rural people need to be integrated within all aspects of sustainable rural development and EFA, through plans of action that are multisectoral and interdisciplinary (FAO/UNESCO-IIEP, 2006b; FAO/UNESCO-IIEP, 2006c).

Message of UN Secretary-General on EFA
25 September 2008

Secretary-General, in message says education can drive economic, social progress; failure to provide education for all puts entire generation at risk

Following is UN Secretary-General Ban Ki-moon's message, as delivered by Ann Veneman, Executive Director of the United Nations Children's Fund, for the event on Education for All, today, in New York:

"I am grateful to the Global Campaign for Education for bringing this diverse group together. We need a genuine spirit of solidarity in order to reach all of the Millennium Development Goals, and it is heartening that leaders from the private sector, academia, the faith community and Governments are coming together here.

If we forge a broad partnership, we can achieve the Millennium Development Goals by the target date of 2015. We have already seen great progress in the area of education. More children are in school than ever before. More girls are getting the equal education that they deserve.

We have to build on this momentum based on the conviction that education can drive economic and social progress.

One of the best investments that any country can make is to educate girls and women – so they can earn more income, improve their family's well being, and show their daughters, in turn, what is possible once you can read and write.

We have ample evidence that education improves individual incomes, economic growth, child and maternal health, resistance to disease and environmental practices. With an education, people flourish. Without it, they remain trapped in poverty.

This has never been more important. Rising food and oil prices and the effects of climate change are hurting the poor most.

We need a holistic approach that promotes education along with health care. Children who are malnourished or sick need food and treatment to succeed at school.

Globally, we need a commitment to equity. Right now, children from poor communities, rural areas and minority groups are almost always struggling to learn under worse conditions than others in society.

If we do not close this gap, we put a whole generation at risk, and we allow problems to fester. But if we ensure that all children get the education they deserve, we put both individuals and countries on a sure footing towards a stable future.

Let us renew our commitment to Education for All as an essential component of human rights, development, justice and peace."

Source: UN Department of Public Information, News and Media Division - SG/SM/11819

CHALLENGES and RESPONSES

INTRODUCTION

fter seven years of experience with the ERP partnership, the most important results have been the establishment of a partnership network, the generation of knowledge, the identification of innovations, the lessons learned by ERP partners related to policy and practices, and the capacity development among policy makers of ministries of education and agriculture in a number of countries. The ERP partnership has established a network bridging policies, programmes, competencies and cooperation among organizations and individuals from the education, agriculture and rural development sectors, including relevant ministries, academia and civil society.

The partnership knowledge products were identified through consultations at regional conferences and through research studies. The following section draws on these knowledge products to present an analysis of the challenges faced by rural people with respect to education, training and capacity development. The section provides innovative responses for policy makers, managers and practitioners seeking to meet these challenges, drawing on experience gained by ERP partners worldwide. Ten challenges are presented accompanied by several case studies that provide options for policy responses. This publication expands the work published in the ERP series and aims to share the richness of examples available from a wide range of stakeholders regardless of affiliation.

CHALLENGE 1
Access to education and training

According to education leaders who deal with rural development programmes, the greatest challenge in serving rural populations is providing ready access to quality education and training for all age groups, at all levels of the education system. Senior government representatives from 11 African countries reiterated the need "to address the gross inequities that marginalize rural people, and in particular access to education by girls and women, working children, people in inaccessible and remote areas, nomadic and pastoral communities, ethnic minorities, the disabled, refugees and displaced persons" (FAO/UNESCO-IIEP, 2006b, p. 12).

The *EFA Global Monitoring Report 2009* indicates that, in 2006, over four out of five out of school children are rural. Given that today's children are the adults of the future, four out of five illiterate adults will be rural. In a knowledge economy, given the direct relation between levels of education and income and productivity, this situation will have implications for sustainable development and food security. Progress on sustainable development and food security depends on rural people developing the competencies and capacities to face the current challenges such as food price fluctuations, climate change, the HIV/AIDS pandemic, avian flu, and others.

While overall access to education in the formal and non-formal education sector depends mainly on government political will to build democratic, inclusive, non-elitist modern societies, access to education is also dependent on several other factors. Hereafter are some of the main factors that differentiate rural and urban access to education.

In accessing non-formal education, population density can impact the efficiency of travel for teachers, trainers and extension staff assigned to rural areas. For youth and adult learners, distance to training centres and literacy or adult education programmes can be a barrier because of the costs in time and money required to travel to the learning site and the opportunity cost deriving from lost working hours. In rural areas, telecommunications, another option suitable for delivering teacher training and technical training, are commonly less developed than in urban areas. Funds designated to ERP may be insufficient to overcome these challenges because policy makers may choose to invest in programmes for which the ratio of trainers to learners is more adequate, the delivery of education and training services is easier and costs are lower also owing to communication infrastructure, and the immediate visibility and political return are higher.

Programmes promoting access to appropriate education and training through non-formal delivery systems for youth and adults have not benefited from the same pace of financing and progress enjoyed by formal education. However, there is a critical need for a growing number of rural youth (well over 50 percent of the total rural population in many developing countries) and adults to benefit from education and training to develop their capacities to address changes and crises and contribute to local and national socio-economic and cultural development. "... education is a key asset determining household ability to access higher return activities (whether in agriculture or outside) and escape poverty" (FAO, 2007b).

From the perspective of formal education, ERP practitioners now have a better understanding of the barriers that prevent children from attending school. For a more detailed analysis of this topic, see FAO/UNESCO-IIEP (2003). Among these barriers is the distance of schools from the residence of school-aged children. Free school transport programmes proved to be successful in contributing to increase access to and retention in school and training programmes of rural people. In sparsely populated rural areas, multi-grade classrooms closer to the residence of students can help make formal education more affordable while reducing travel times and gender imbalances (UNESCO-IIEP, 2003). Hunger also poses a significant barrier to regular school attendance. An effective mechanism for improving access, retention and completion rates and readiness to learn is the provision of meals for learners. School feeding programmes can have a dramatic effect. According to a joint report of the World Food Programme (WFP) and the International Food Policy Research Institute (IFPRI) on a programme in Bangladesh, school feeding significantly increases rates of enrolment and attendance, and reduces drop-out. School feeding has raised school enrolment by 14.2 percent and increased school attendance by 1.3 days per month. It has also reduced the probability of dropping out of school by 7.5 percent (IFPRI, 2004).

Other important barriers to formal primary school attendance of rural people have been lowered through the removal or the reduction of school fees, free access to learning materials and school uniforms and, to a lesser extent, school construction in rural areas. According to UNESCO (2008), from 1999 to 2004, Sub-Saharan Africa raised its average net enrolment ratio by 26 percent for an annual increase six times higher than during the decade before Dakar. The increase in South and West Asia was also impressive, rising by 11 percent. However, there is still much work to be done. There are still countries where net enrolment rates of primary school age children are below 60 percent. Children from poor households often do not attend school or face major obstacles in access to good quality education (UNESCO, 2008; UN Millennium Project, 2005). The ADEA (Association for the Development of Education in Africa) 2008 Biennale on post-primary education highlighted the lack of opportunities for rural people to continue their studies at further levels of education, and the need for policy makers to address such gap was recommended.

CHALLENGE ①

An example from India:
private sector-government partnership to provide millions of school meals

Organizations: Government of India, Deshpande Foundation, Akshaya Patra Foundation

Source: http://commitments.clintonglobalinitiative.org/projects.htm?status=1&category=50&sort_order=DESC&sort_by=lastactivity&start=24

In January 2008, an innovative school feeding programme was launched in India with the goal of providing meals to over 200 million school children every year. The objective is to develop a long-term sustainable programme supported by government, private donors and individuals so that Indian school children from kindergarten to grade 10 will receive at least one nutritious meal every day. The programme is currently operating in Karnataka, Uttar Pradesh, Rajasthan, Orissa and Gujarat.

The programme is made possible through a partnership between the Deshpande Foundation of Andover, Massachusetts, Unites States of America (USA), the Akshaya Patra Foundation in India and the Government of India's Midday Meal Programme. The Deshpande Foundation, a fairly young organization established in the United States in 1996, supports work in the areas of innovation, entrepreneurship and international development. The Deshpande Foundation made a grant to fund the construction of the largest kitchen for the programme and provides other support to the Akshaya Patra Foundation, considered "a new model for NGOs in India". Akshaya Patra currently runs the world's largest school feeding programme.

The programme now provides meals to over 800 000 children on a daily basis. Most of the food is prepared in 11 large, centralized kitchens. The kitchens are so efficient they can prepare over 100 000 meals in less than five hours with minimum labour and maximum sustained quality. The kitchen for the Hubli District of Karnataka, considered the largest in the world, has the capacity to cook almost 200 000 meals every day. The programme uses an innovative design for its kitchens and an efficient supply chain taking advantage of locally grown produce from village farmers. The food is delivered by trucks throughout the school districts, including rural areas. The food is packed in stainless steel containers and shipped in heat-insulated, dust-free special purpose vehicles.

The programme has also a special component for remote rural schools where groups of women are trained in hygiene and nutrition to cook lunches on a daily basis while maintaining the same high standards of quality that are required at the certified central kitchens. These smaller kitchens in rural areas are able to feed around 600 children a day.

School meals are an important link between education and a child's health. In India, more than 40 million children are affected by malnutrition and related ailments like anaemia and diarrhoea. For many children, lunch at school is the main meal of the day, providing up to 40 percent of the daily micronutrient needs. Studies in both the city of Bangalore and rural villages of Rajasthan have shown that school meals contribute to substantially higher school attendance, especially among girls, and improved learning ability.

An example from Bolivia:
overcoming educational barriers for isolated rural communities

Organizations: People's Foundation, W.K. Kellogg Foundation, municipal governments

Source: http://www.wkkf.org/default.aspx?tabid=94&CID=145&NID=85&ItemID=5001013&LanguageID=0

Second place winner of the 2006/2007 cycle of the Experiences in Social Innovation Award organized by the United Nations Economic Commission for Latin America and the Caribbean (ECLAC), the Student Family Lodging Programme of the People's Foundation of Bolivia has demonstrated considerable success in enabling young people from extremely poor families living in isolated communities in the highlands of Bolivia to attend school on a regular basis.

Beginning as a fairly small project 10 years ago, now the programme has over 280 students from the municipal districts of Yanacachi, Llallagua, Pocoata and Colquecha. Sustainability for this model is assured by the financial support from municipal governments that have signed agreements with the People's Foundation, guaranteeing funding from their annual budgets.

The Andean Region of Bolivia is characterized by a low development index and a large number of isolated communities. School drop-out rates in the Andean Highlands are among the highest in the country. In northern Potosi, only 58.5 percent of the schools have classes beyond grade 3. Distances between communities and schools that offer education up to the mandatory grade 8 are an average of 11 kilometres – a two-hour walk for children.

The programme consists of establishing educational centres in strategically located villages allowing youth from neighbouring communities easier access to school. The initiative has also an accommodation network of host families. During the week, young people focus on their studies and participate in regular capacity building seminars on nutrition, hygiene and health. On the weekends, they return to their homes. As an on-going part of the programme, teachers receive regular training to improve the quality of instruction.

Interestingly, the programme is based on an ancestral custom of the Aymara people, an indigenous group in Bolivia, referred to as *utawawa*. Families living far away from a school would send their children to live with relatives or godparents to study. The problem was that in exchange for room and board, the young person was expected to carry out significant domestic and agricultural chores. While providing some children with an education, this tradition contributed to child labour.

Under the current Student Family Lodging Programme, the quality of services provided by the host families is closely supervised by staff from each educational centre. The rights of the students include their own bed, proper meals and clean hygienic living conditions. The programme has clearly demonstrated that it has the capacity to help students improve their academic performance and raise the number of children enrolled in school. Without having to work to pay for their studies and having their basic needs met, most students have obtained good academic results.

The ECLAC Award Programme Judging Committee said that the Student Family Lodging Programme stands out for the scale of its accomplishments: a significant improvement in school access, attendance and completion of primary education, promotion of school attendance by girls and contribution to the Millennium Development Goals of universal primary education and gender equality in primary and secondary education.

CHALLENGE 2
Quality of education and training

The quality of education and training available in rural areas lags behind the quality of urban areas. Yet, quality remains a critical foundational aspect of any advance in ERP. The quality of education and training depends on many factors like the quality of existing facilities such as schools, boarding schools and training centres; the qualifications of extension workers and teachers and their proficiency; the quality of teaching and training materials; and the use of formative evaluation for continuous improvement. Other factors include leadership to ensure that resources are provided on a long-term basis and that motivation is maintained, a curriculum developed for the specific audience, and strong links to community for support. Relevance of education and training is vital to increasing the appeal and utility for rural people. Contextualized learning allows learners of all ages to study, solve real-life problems and acquire life skills (FAO/UNESCO-IIEP, 2003). When curriculum, learning materials and learning methods are designed to be relevant to rural realities, the perceived quality and utility of education improves among parents and students.

Non-formal education is seldom compulsory. Thus, relevance of non-formal education and training is of paramount importance for young and adult rural learners. Rural citizens "vote with their feet" and may simply choose not to return for follow-up education and training sessions if the perceived quality and relevance of the service delivered are low.

In some cases, flexibility is foreseen to allow local content in education and training. Programmes that utilize participatory curriculum development at local levels (districts and regions) combined with central national curriculum planning can have far greater appeal than purely centrally backed programmes (FAO, 2002b).

Education and training that allow rural citizens to adjust to new realities and trends, such as health and market challenges, climate change and sustainable natural resource management will serve the best interests of the learners. One challenge associated with new realities and trends is that learners may not immediately appreciate the relevance of training and education on such topics.

31

EFA National Plans have been successful in bringing millions of additional students into classrooms when compared to a decade ago. Aggressive action will need to be taken to ensure rural students greater inclusion, retention and completion of basic education as well as their continuation at the different levels of the education system. Maintaining high quality education is certainly part of the formula for retaining students in school. Educational innovations are also crucial to maintaining quality. For example, school gardening programmes have been used effectively to increase relevance and quality while teaching language, mathematics, science, agriculture and entrepreneurship.

An example from Honduras:
alternative education reaching youth and adults in rural areas

Organizations: Educatodos, USAID, Government of Honduras, municipalities, NGOs, private sector

Source: http://www.educatodos.hn/ and http://www.comminit.com/en/node/149305

Created in 1996, *Educatodos* was a response by the Secretary of Education of Honduras to find a way to reach out of school youth and ensure that both young people and adults complete at least grade 6 as part of the country's EFA goals. Surveys indicate that there were approximately 540 000 students who had dropped out of school and an additional 1.1 million young adults aged between 19 and 30 who failed to complete nine years of basic education. There were also indications that many adults were interested in seeking an alternative means of acquiring a basic education. The overall goal of the programme was to increase economic participation and income of the poor by expanding access to high quality basic education for out of school youth and adults.

With the assistance of USAID and additional support provided by municipal governments, private voluntary organizations and businesses, *Educatodos* was designed to cost-effectively respond to the demand for basic education in a significantly shorter time frame than the traditional education system. The programme started as an opportunity for youth and adults in isolated rural areas to complete grades 1 through 6 in only three years. In 2000, the programme expanded to include grades 7 to 9 and now enrols annually about 80 000 young people and adults with two periods of instruction each year.

Educatodos classes meet in existing public and private buildings at the community level, like factories, businesses, schools, churches and community centres. The curriculum is presented through interactive radio in an integrated way incorporating both printed and audio materials. Over 4 000 volunteer facilitators with different academic backgrounds implement the programme at the learning centres. The educational content is based on the National Curriculum for Basic Education.

In 2001, a study carried out by researchers from the Universidad Pedagógica Nacional Francisco Morozán measured learning, comparing *Educatodos* students and pupils from the traditional national education system. The findings indicated that students from *Educatodos* demonstrated similar and, in some cases, better performance in subjects such as Spanish and mathematics than students in the regular public school system. It indicated that these results were achieved even though they had fewer resources, spent less time in school and had volunteer facilitators instead of teachers.

Through documentation, the programme has been able to estimate that the additional years of schooling have increased earnings of all *Educatodos* graduates over the years by more than US$ 250 millions. Other benefits obtained from the participation in *Educatodos* included: improvements in family health; increased acceptance and use of family planning; reduction in primary school drop-out and grade repetition rates for the children of *Educatodos* participants; and increased civic participation.

An example from India:
mobile laboratories bring exciting science education to the doorstep of classrooms across rural areas

Organizations: Agastya International Foundation, Give2Asia, Government of India

Source: http://www.agastya.org/aboutus.htm and http://www.give2asia.org/page12021.cfm

Agastya International is an NGO led by entrepreneurs, educators, scientists, teachers and children with the purpose of transforming and revitalizing primary and secondary education in India, including rural villages. They have developed a model for science education that is affordable and can be replicated anywhere in the world.

CHALLENGE ②

So far, Agastya has reached over 70 000 teachers and 2 million children with the programme.

In India, especially in rural villages, uninspiring, rote-based learning is still the prevailing educational methodology, which does not equip poor rural children with the necessary tools to overcome poverty. As a global IT power, the Government of India continues to focus educational resources on the relatively small group of urban-based engineers and scientists, largely ignoring the biggest population component – rural communities that lack adequate primary and secondary education. Among children under the age of 15, it is estimated that still 13 millions are not enrolled in school; most of them are girls and live in rural areas.

With the financial support of Give2Asia, the Agastya International Foundation created and implemented an innovative educational programme using mobile science laboratories. The mobile science lab units have covered thousands of kilometres to reach even remote schools throughout the southern states of Andhra Pradesh, Karnataka and Tamil Nadu. Each mobile lab reaches around 30 000 students a year.

The programme has 30 minibuses equipped with folding tables, projection screens and experimental models. The sessions are carried out in the villages in school buildings, under the trees or in the open air during good weather. Not only does the programme attract school children and their teachers, but also parents, day labourers and other villagers often participate. The mobile science labs visit most schools on a weekly basis over a period of several weeks to maintain some level of continuity.

Over 120 fun and simple experiments have been developed to explain and demonstrate varied scientific principles. The experiments often use easily found low-cost everyday materials and supplies. The learning is hands-on and deductive, encouraging creative thinking and problem solving.

As an example, in one experiment, each child is blindfolded and given a small cup of water to taste and distinguish a plain, salty and sweet liquid. In this way, children learn about the link between the brain and the senses. Another experiment uses a rolled-up newspaper to simulate a makeshift telescope and demonstrate the concept of refraction, while a shoebox is used to explain how a camera works.

The programme usually involves from 50 to 100 children per session. The teams of specialists spend from two to three hours at each location and the lessons usually take 45 minutes to an hour. A travelling team can visit two to three schools a day depending on the distances between schools. The mobile teams also periodically bring science fairs to the countryside where they recruit 14 to 16 year old student volunteers to lead science experiments with younger children.

Evaluations of the programme have indicated there has been a great deal of change in the attitudes students have about learning. Children and parents seem to take a new interest in school and education in general. Teachers have become more motivated and are applying new ways of teaching as a result of observing the more interactive learning approaches used by the mobile science labs.

CHALLENGE 3
Decentralization and community involvement

Governments embrace varying degrees of decentralization in decision-making and resource distribution. In some cases, decentralization is viewed as a cost-saving measure and a way to reduce the size of central bureaucracies. In other cases, it is considered as a way to make services more effective as the decision-making chain is shortened and actions are increasingly relevant to local circumstances. The same applies to education, training, and capacity development.

Decentralization is one response to more traditional, centrally controlled national education systems. When decentralization is combined with greater flexibility in formal and non-formal curricula and local control over content, the results have been promising. An increased level of community engagement with education and training programmes is one benefit of locally controlled education decision-making. Education and training systems that combine centrally planned curricula with some local content determined through community input have proven successful in several tests. In Thailand, for example, as much as 40 percent of the curriculum was allowed to be based on community and local needs (FAO/UNESCO-IIEP, 2002).

Other forms of flexibility play a role in increasing access to training and education. For example, non-formal training and school schedules may need to be flexible to accommodate weather, cropping patterns and the movement of nomads (Acker and Gasperini, 2008; ADB/UNESCO-IIEP, 2005). Some local control of formal education processes may allow such accommodations as local languages to be used as the medium of instruction through the middle primary grades. It may also permit flexibility in terms of modest delays in the entry age of children who live in remote areas and must travel long distances to attend school. Engagement of communities may also lead to the engagement of other community resource people to teach skills that extension staff and teachers may not know.

Decentralization can be a first step to greater community involvement. Participatory and community-based approaches to school management and curriculum development have increased community ownership of schools, which is one factor leading to increased

CHALLENGE ③

enrolments (FAO/UNESCO-IIEP, 2006b). Rural families need to see that the education their children receive is relevant, that the school is a safe environment, and that proper supervision of the institution is provided. The development of parent–teacher organizations can have a significant impact on resources available to the school, as well as on improved monitoring of quality, relevance, and such critically important supporting elements as school feeding programmes. With better school and community cooperation come opportunities for integrating learning that combines classroom and community-based learning (FAO/UNESCO-IIEP, 2005a).

School gardens or school-based rural radio can be used as two different ways of promoting community involvement.

Local involvement in and control over the learning enterprise is critical to success. At an ERP workshop held in Bangkok in 2002, this process of community empowerment was referred to as moving from "donorship to ownership".

Decentralization also has a darker side. It has been used by central governments as an excuse for shifting funds away from ERP into education services that favour the elite by providing free education to urban dwellers while simultaneously offering education on a cost-sharing basis to rural people. Cost-sharing policies, frequently recommended by structural adjustment interventions, have resulted in decreased access to education and training by poor communities. In 2000, the World Bank, acknowledging the perverse effect of cost-sharing policies in increasing access to basic education services, reconsidered its own policies and withdrew from recommending cost-sharing in basic education.

With regard to non-formal education, community learning centres in remote communities can provide basic education including skills training, environmental education, and health and HIV/AIDS education (FAO/UNESCO-IIEP, 2005a). Such centres can be as simple as a primary school used as an adult education facility after hours.

CHALLENGE ③

An example from Cambodia:
community involvement key to quality education in rural areas
Organizations: World Education, EQUIP1, Ministry of Education, Youth and Sports

Source: http://www.worlded.org/WEIInternet/features/cambodia_rural_communities.cfm

Although the Cambodian constitution guarantees the right to basic education for all children in the country, there is a gap between policy and reality. Barriers to quality basic education, especially in remote rural areas, include low educational relevance, teacher shortages, limited financial resources, long distances to available schools and a low perceived importance of education among parents and the community in general.

In some rural areas, there are inadequate school facilities and it is difficult to recruit teachers because of the poor living and working conditions in the villages. Most families cannot afford school fees and the cost of supplies. Cambodian families in rural areas prefer to keep their children at home, especially girls, to help take care of younger siblings and do house chores.

The Educational Support for Children of Underserved Populations (ESCUP) programme was designed to increase the access and improve the quality of basic education in rural communities. ESCUP is being implemented in the provinces of Kampong, Cham, Kratie, and Mondulkiri with technical support from World Education, the American Institute for Research and EQUIP1 in a cooperative agreement with USAID and the Ministry of Education, Youth and Sports. The areas of intervention include: teacher education, educational access and quality, and school-community partnerships.

In the village of Chour Krang, in the northeast province of Kratie, children from the Steang minority group had to walk almost four kilometres every day through dense bush and forest to reach their school. The education of younger children was delayed because of the long distances to school. There was a similar access problem for the children of Beoung Char, an island in the middle of the Mekong River along the border of Kratie Province. Families are spread out over the 15-kilometre island that lacked proper roads. Although there were three schools on the island, they were too far away for most of the children to attend.

To help solve some of the problems, World Education and its partners started to form school committees made up of teachers, parents and village leaders. With support from the ESCUP project, community members worked together to find solutions and take the necessary action. In Chour Krang, community members worked together to build a temporary school building closer to the village. ESCUP provided the funds for materials and the community provided labour. As a result of this activity, parents and village leaders are more involved and engaged in keeping their children in school. More than 113 children are now attending the school. Children are able to enrol at the age of six because of the reduced walk to go to school. The community and teachers now work together to identify out of school youth and help them go back to school.

CHALLENGE 3

In Beoung Char, the school committee that was formed worked together to build several small schools in areas far from the existing government schools. It was then difficult to find teachers who were willing to live and work in these remote areas. ESCUP worked with the community to identify local community members and train them as teachers. This resulted in a success, as the teachers coming from the local communities better understand the children and their situation. In Cambodia, ESCUP has facilitated better communication and collaboration between the communities, the schools and the Ministry of Education, Youth and Sports and has strengthened the role of the community in promoting quality education for their children.

An example from China:
community-based environmental education curriculum created to complement primary education in rural areas

Organizations: Rural China Education Foundation, Green Watershed, Brooks,
Lashi Hai Nature Reserve, Bureau of Education

Source: http://www.ruralchina.org/site/index.php?option=com_content&task=view&id=72&Itemid=113

Working with local schools, the Native Soil Education Project represents an effort by the Rural China Education Foundation to enrich the national curriculum with a non-formal education lesson plan adapted to local interests and needs.

The project took place in the Lashi Township of Yunnan Province, in southern China, an environmentally important area called the Lashi Hai Watershed where the Yangtze and the Lancang Rivers merge at Lashi Lake. The water flows out of the lake and forms the Mekong River that goes through five countries, eventually entering the South China Sea.

The watershed includes one of the few highland wetlands in the country and has a rich biological and cultural diversity. Most of the people belong to one of the two ethnic minority groups – the Naxi and the Yi. Traditional work activities include fishing the waters of Lashi Lake, farming and employment as government loggers.

In the 1990s, a series of ineffective government policies and the construction of a dam left communities in the area stricken by poverty, and ethnic minorities were even more disadvantaged. The dam severely damaged the local ecosystem and destroyed farmland. The government then declared Lake Lashi a protected wetland preserve and allowed no fishing. In 1998, the government banned logging in the Province – good for the environment, but devastating to the local economy and to the loggers who depended on this income.

Thanks to the government and two NGOs – Green Watershed and Brooks – the situation is improving. Communities in the watershed are becoming involved and take greater responsibility in managing the natural resources of the area. To support this effort, the Native Soil Education Project was designed to foster children's appreciation of their home, their culture and the surrounding natural environment. It helps them

CHALLENGE ③

understand the drastic changes that recently took place in their area, and gives them the skills and knowledge to contribute to the sustainable development of their community both now and in the future.

The curriculum development process started in November 2006. Community members participated, and most content of the curriculum comes from the local community like for example indigenous literature and art, life stories from community members, and familiar places and scenes from students' everyday lives. After extensive community consultations, the project team and local teachers spent months writing the textbook and accompanying activities.

The text, I Love Lashi Hai, is being used in the classes of grades 3 and 4 and encourages enquiry and exploration. The project promotes learning methods that encourage students to learn about and contribute to the development of their local communities. Lessons include simulations and enquiry activities that facilitate experiential learning and give the students the tools to take action. During summer vacation, teachers from the school are invited to a local camp where they learn and practice participatory activities based on the curriculum. The curriculum is new, but the initial feedback from the school is very positive.

An example from Nepal:
community-managed school in rural areas

Organizations: World Bank, Centre for Community Development and Research (CCODER), UNDP, World Food Programme, UNICEF

Source: http://www.irinnews.org/report.aspx?reportid=28862 and http://www.ccoder.org/com_school.htm

Over the years, there have been serious problems with ERP in Nepal. Nepal's literacy rate is one of the lowest in the world, while the school drop-out rate for children has been one of the highest (70 percent). Schools are generally inadequate with poorly maintained facilities and teachers who are not qualified or committed. The Maoist insurgency, that is pervasive throughout the country, has been particularly disruptive to education, especially in rural areas.

As a way to improve quality and access to education and make progress toward the Millennium Development Goals, the government, with the encouragement of the international development and donor community, charted a course of action to gradually transfer responsibility for education to local communities. The legal groundwork for community-managed schools was laid out in the 1999 Local Self-Governance Act. The first transfers took place in 2002 when 95 schools were handed over to community management. By 2006, over 2 200 previously government-run schools in 62 of the 75 districts in the country had been turned over to local communities.

To be successful, this large-scale reform requires the assistance of international development organizations and agencies, as well as national and local NGOs. There are several initiatives supported by the various development agencies and NGOs, including the Community School Support Programme (CSSP), funded by the World Bank; the Community-Owned Primary School (COPE) assisted by UNDP-supported projects, World Food Programme, UNICEF and UNFPA; and the Community Schools supported by

the Centre for Community Development and Research (CCODER). In most cases, the government provides a one-time grant of US$ 1 500 to schools that are to be managed by the local community. After this initial grant, schools are completely independent with no further influence from the government.

The management arrangements are somewhat different depending on the supporting organization or agency. For example, the CSSP schools are jointly managed by teachers, parents, community leaders and a regional organization, the Regional Community Development Committee (RCDC). The regional organization is a federation of several village-level organizations called Community Development Committees (CDC). Each CDC sends representatives to the regional Community Education Committee (CEC). The CEC, along with teachers and parents, is responsible for the organization, supervision and control of all school matters. In this way, the schools are managed with maximum community participation and ownership. For example, the CEC has the power to hire and dismiss teachers who fail to reach the required standards.

The educational reform has met with many challenges and controversies. The Nepal National Teachers Association, with its 80 000 members, is against the reform. Teachers are concerned about giving responsibility for their supervision, hiring and firing to local communities. The Maoists want the government to take back the education system, accusing the state of running away from its responsibilities.

All indications are that, considering the extremely poor performance of schools under government administration, the community-based school reform is working. In 2007, the Nepalese news portal Katiput reported that in the 500 community schools in Ilam District more girls than boys were enrolled. Evaluations from the World Bank's International Development Association found in a survey of 30 selected community schools covering 10 000 households that the number of out of school children (5 to 9 years of age) decreased from 41 to 15 percent and out of school girls from 42 to 15 percent. Other findings were that there was increased community ownership and participation indicated by a higher number of School Management Committee meetings, increased resource generation and more frequent parent visits to schools. There were also many transfers of children from private schools to community schools, reduced teacher absenteeism and an improved learning environment.

CHALLENGE 4
Gender-responsive learning environments

The barriers to full participation in education and training for rural adult women, female youth and primary school-aged girls are numerous and well documented. Labour requirements associated with agricultural and household tasks, cultural barriers, lack of well-supervised boarding facilities, sexual harassment and a range of gender equity issues constitute a few of the barriers to greater participation. Unfortunately, gender barriers to training and education in rural areas are typically more pronounced than those in urban areas (FAO/UNESCO-IIEP, 2006b).

At the same time, there is strong evidence that points to the very positive social returns on investments in education and training for girls and women. In *Higher agricultural education and opportunities in rural development for women* (FAO, 1997, preface) the following statement appeared:

"From a developmental perspective, investing in the education of females has the highest rate of return of any possible investment in developing countries".

To attract and retain female learners requires some accommodations. Flexible timetables to accommodate peak labour demand for children, youth and adults have helped to increase attendance in some schools and at farmer training events. In situations where the training centres or schools are distant from the learners' homes, secure and well-supervised boarding facilities have shown to be critical in safeguarding the well-being of participants and in inspiring confidence among family members who may control decisions about women's participation. Security and privacy for girls, such as separate toilets, are also important factors (UN Millennium Project, 2005). Access to water for personal hygiene is also an important factor in the attendance of teenage girl students.

In formal school settings there are a number of innovations that have proven effective. Take-home rations for female children can compensate for the labour lost when they attend school (FAO/UNESCO-IIEP, 2006b). Direct conditional fund transfers to families to reward school attendance, such as *Bolsa Escola* (and later *Bolsa Familia*) in Brazil, demonstrated high rates of return. Use of female teachers helps to ensure a safer school environment as well as providing a role model for female students (FAO/UNESCO-IIEP, 2002). Reduction in gender stereotyping in curricula can improve the classroom environment (UN Millennium Project 2005). While this applies in general, it is even more critical in addressing the stereotyped profiles of rural women and men, where inequality and inequity are reinforced. Legislation and/or school rules against sexual harassment and sexual violence help to send a clear message about behavioural expectations.

An example from Burkina Faso: girl-friendly schools see enrolments soar

Organizations: USAID, Plan International

Source: http://www.plan-international.org/news/bright/

Thousands of girls in Burkina Faso, who would not be going to school, are now receiving an education thanks to a project implemented by Plan International with financial support from the USAID-Millennium Challenge Corporation. The project called BRIGHT (Burkinabé Response to Improve Girls Chances to Succeed) has achieved high levels of school enrolment and graduation rates by creating supportive learning environments in 132 communities in 10 provinces.

In Burkina Faso, 73 percent of all girls never finish primary school. Many of them are forced to stay home to look after their younger brothers and sisters, and do chores around the house while their parents work in the fields. An important reason for girls not attending school is the lack of private latrines on school grounds. As part of a larger global study, Plan International estimates that Burkina Faso will experience a net growth loss valued at US$ 75 millions by not improving education for girls in the country.

The BRIGHT project works with local governments and communities to support child-friendly classrooms. In Burkina Faso, school management committees are formed to empower young people and communities to have a greater say in what happens in their local school. The communities involved in the project have been able to acquire furniture and textbooks for classrooms and dig wells to provide safe drinking water for students and teachers.

An improvement that has probably led to the most significant increase in enrolment, retention and graduation rates among girls has been the construction of separate male and female latrine blocks. The new facilities also have arrangements for sanitary hand washing. As part of the project, students and community members are taught about sanitation and personal hygiene. An aspect of the project that has contributed to the successful recruitment and retention of good teachers has been the building of houses for teachers in the community. The facilities and buildings were built by the community using local materials.

The project provides a midday meal for all students and, as an additional incentive, girls who attend 90 percent or more of the time are given a take-home ration of food. Some of the schools also have child care centres that allow mothers to leave their youngest children under safe supervision so that their older daughters can go to school while they work in the fields. Plan International reports that in many communities where the project was implemented, enrolment has far exceeded original estimates and some classrooms now have more girls than boys.

An example from Cambodia:
home counselling helps keep girls in school

Organizations: Ministry of Education, Youth and Sports, UNICEF

Source: http://www.unicef.org/infobycountry/cambodia_39364.html

As in many other countries, girls in Cambodia tend to drop out of school when they reach the upper grade levels of primary education. This is especially true for rural areas of the country. There is no gender gap in grade 1, but by grade 7, a significant percentage of girls have already left school.

Cambodia has come a long way in improving education since schools were abolished during the Khmer Rouge regime, but many parents do not appreciate the value of education. Especially in rural areas, it is difficult for them to see evidence of economic opportunities as a result of their children going to school. Parents often want their daughters to help with household chores, work beside them in the fields tending crops

or contribute to the family income by working in the garment factories, instead of going to school.

Although new schools are being built, teachers trained and enrolment has been increasing over the years, secondary school participation is low and the gender gap is wide. Only around 30 percent of the boys and 10 percent of the girls go on to secondary education.

Gender responsiveness is one of the key components of a comprehensive new programme called the Child-Friendly Schools Initiative carried out by the Ministry of Education, Youth and Sports and supported by UNICEF. The overall purpose of the programme is to improve the quality of basic education and assure equitable access to schools.

Home counselling is combined with a community research component to identify gender-related barriers to education and determine how to increase awareness about gender equality. The child-friendly schools reach out to girls and their families who are at risk of dropping out of school.

In participating schools, female teachers and/or volunteer mothers are identified to serve as "girl counsellors". The programme targets girls in grades 5 and 6. Classroom teachers inform a counsellor when a female student misses more than three days of school. The counsellor visits the home of the student to discuss the problem and to identify with the student and her parents the underlying causes for dropping out. Appropriate solutions are identified and agreed upon by the student and her parents.

The home counselling initiative is meeting with considerable success. Evaluation studies indicate that many girls return to school after having experienced home counselling with their parents. There is still considerable work to be done, as even after home counselling, some girls do not return to school and others drop out again.

CHALLENGE 5
Organizational and institutional efficiency

In situations where public resources are severely limited, ERP programmes need to find ways to optimize their organizational efficiency. No single institution is in the position to provide all the necessary educational services in rural areas. One logical approach is to think systemically about the array of rural actors that could be better coordinated to optimize education programme delivery.

Coordination is needed at the macro institutional level, between ministries of education, youth and agriculture, as well as at micro levels, in schools and training centres and courses, between the education and training providers and the communities and learners. An example of interministerial collaboration is the Kosovo Strategy for ERP (MEST/MAFRD/FAO, 2004), prepared with FAO technical assistance. The strategy was instrumental to leveraging donor funding such as OSCE (Organization for Security and Co-operation in Europe) funding for improving the quality of education by enhancing curriculum relevance to rural people's needs.

One particularly attractive area for identifying organizational efficiencies is that of coordination among education-oriented providers such as extension workers, schools, non-governmental organizations, and the private sector. For example, trained agricultural extension agents who are already located in rural areas are a valuable potential resource for making presentations in their subject area at local schools, for conducting adult basic education classes when farmers gather for technical training, and for organizing farmer field schools that involve both technical and basic education outcomes. Similarly teachers, if trained in specific technical subjects, can support extension programmes during non-teaching hours, if appropriate incentives are provided.

Extension is an important aspect of ERP. Yet, it is often neglected as an education programme because typically it is not managed by the ministry of education. Fundamentally, effective extension serves an education as well as a communication function in relaying user needs back to researchers and policy makers. A similar situation of neglect affects most rural youth and adult education and training activities such as literacy and skills training which are beyond the immediate responsibility of ministries of education. The lack

of institutionalized interministerial collaboration explains the slow path in achieving the EFA goals for reducing adult illiteracy and reaffirms the urgency for concerted intersectoral and interinstitutional programmes for rural youth and adults.

Farmers Field Schools (FFS) and school garden programmes are examples of interministerial collaboration by which governments, often with FAO technical assistance, are reaching out rural youth and adults in non-formal education and children at the primary school level. Such programmes contribute to prepare future farmers while teaching about language, mathematics, drawing, science, agriculture, environment, and in some cases, entrepreneurship. FFS and gardens are often a joint programme between teachers and extension workers.

55

Another approach is to look for greater financial efficiency in existing programmes. Reducing costs may be possible in the formal education sector through the use of low-cost school construction methods (UN Millennium Project, 2005). Promoting school networks or clusters can achieve efficiencies through the sharing of equipment and other specialized resources. Lastly, capacity development for head teachers and extension leaders can lay the foundation for improvements in education and training management efficiency in rural areas.

Education and training facilities represent a significant public investment in rural areas. Given the initial capital costs as well as the recurring maintenance costs of such infrastructure, it is only reasonable to explore options that optimize efficiency. Better utilization of limited school infrastructure can be achieved through such ideas as double-shift classes and/or utilization of the classrooms for after-hours adult education or extension workshops. Given that rural school transport is too costly to consider for many highly indebted poor countries, feeder or lower primary satellite schools can accommodate the youngest children in remote areas until they are strong enough to walk longer distances to a proper primary school.

An example from Bangladesh:
Rural Advancement Committee non-formal primary education opens
schooling to millions in rural villages

Organizations: BRAC and local NGOs

Source: http://www.brac.net/

BRAC, formally the Bangladesh Rural Advancement Committee, is the largest local non-governmental organization in the world. It has developed a non-formal primary education programme that in 1999 operated more than 35 000 schools in rural Bangladesh with over one million children enrolled. Over 66 percent of the students are girls and among the teachers, 97 percent are female. These schools serve the poorest of the rural poor who, for one reason or another, are not able to enter the formal government education system. BRAC provides financial and technical support to 284 small NGOs throughout the country to implement the programme.

Although academically comparable to the formal system, BRAC's schooling is considered non-formal because the schools are not permanent institutions and the teachers are not formally trained in the traditional sense. The schools, targeting children in rural villages between the ages of 8 and 10, are organized around a group of 30 students. These students advance together through the three to four-year programme. After that period, the school ceases to exist unless there is another group from the community of at least 30 students to enrol and form a new school. For the students and their families, there are no fees and BRAC assumes all the costs of supplies.

The one-room schools are in session for two-and-a-half to three hours a day, six days a week for 268 days per year. The typical school is a room in a house or store that is rented for three hours a day. Generally, the walls are made of bamboo and mud with packed dirt floors. Students sit in a circle on mats holding slate boards on their knees. The teacher has a metal stool and a metal truck that doubles as a desk and a place to store supplies.

Uniforms are not required and school hours vary according to home and agricultural cycle needs. Schools are located no more than two kilometres from students' homes.

CHALLENGE ⑤

Parents are required to attend monthly meetings and promise to send their children to school. Together, parents are encouraged, within the guidelines, to make recommendations related to the general operations of the school, including time of day for school sessions.

Almost all teacher-trainees are rural women who must have completed at least nine years of schooling. These paraprofessionals start teaching in a first grade, multi-age classroom with only 15 days of initial basic teacher training. They are supported by monthly refresher courses and continuous close supervision by BRAC staff. Weekly visits by BRAC field staff provide regular feedback. These teachers proved to deliver primary education that equals or exceeds primary education provided by government-funded formal system.

An example from Kosovo:
national strategy for education for rural people developed by participatory action

Organizations: Ministry of Education, Science and Technology, Ministry of Agriculture, Forestry and Rural Development, NGOs, municipalities, FAO

Source: Draft FAO document: Participatory Strategy Development for Education for Rural People in Kosovo

As a disputed territory, Kosovo suffered greatly during the 1990s when Serbia abolished its autonomy. With an already existing weak economy, the situation further deteriorated owing to a combination of poor economic policies, international sanctions, limited external commerce and ethnic conflict. During that time, education for the ethnic majority Albanians was abolished, forcing them to create a parallel education system that resulted in large inequalities, especially in rural areas characterized by high levels of illiteracy and large skills gaps and where 60 percent of the people live.

The new Ministry of Education, Science and Technology (MEST) and the Ministry of Agriculture, Forestry and Rural Development (MAFRD) were established after parliamentary elections in 2002. The government set as one of its priorities the support of rural development and the promotion of employment and sustainable livelihoods for the rural population. Basic education and skills development are considered critical to the development of rural populations.

In 2003, MEST and MAFRD requested FAO technical assistance to develop a national strategy for Education of Rural People and at the same time develop capacities of government staff within the two ministries. To support the development of the national strategy in a participatory manner, MEST and MAFRD staff gained skills around three main stages of intervention: (1) planning, (2) needs assessment and (3) strategy formulation.

To facilitate the participatory development of the strategy, a broad base of local and central stakeholders was involved in the process, including the Project Team, a Strategy Formulation Team (SFT) and Local Task Teams (LTT). The Project Team, composed of one national and one international education planning specialist and one specialist in human resources development, guided the overall implementation of the project.

The SFT developed the methodology and overall work plan for the project. It included representation from various ministries of government, school directors and teachers, local NGOs; individual, groups and organizations from selected villages; and representatives from the LTTs.

The LTTs were formed from selected stakeholder groups at the village level including school personnel, farmers and women associations. Their tasks were to facilitate and assist with the assessment process at the local level thus contributing to the work of the SFT and to represent their stakeholder views at the various workshops.

The assessment process took six months and resulted in policy recommendations which formed the basis of the strategy formulation. Local and provincial workshops were organized to present and discuss the findings with a broader audience.

Strategy formulation included three steps: (1) definition of vision and strategic goals; (2) identification of objectives and necessary action; and (3) converting strategy into a programme of action. The resulting medium term strategy (2004-2009) included eight goals and subsequent lines of action for improving the quality of ERP in Kosovo. In addition to the strategic plan, 21 staff members of MEST and municipal personnel were trained in participatory planning and strategy development (MEST/MAFRD/FAO, 2004).

The ERP National Strategy was submitted to donors and drove government and international support to foster access to and quality of education and training for rural people.

CHALLENGE (5)

59

An example from Uganda:
trained community volunteers support agriculture and nutrition extension
Organizations: Volunteer Efforts for Development Concerns, Makerere University and Iowa State University

Source: http://www.srl.ag.iastate.edu/

The Center for Sustainable Rural Livelihoods (CSRL) of the College of Agriculture and Life Sciences at Iowa State University leads a rural development programme in central Uganda in partnership with a local non-governmental organization, Volunteers Efforts for Development Concerns (VEDCO), and the Faculty of Agriculture of Makerere University. The intended outcome of this programme is that rural people will have access to sufficient food, sustainable incomes and livelihoods that result in good health and well-being. To achieve these outcomes, the programme engages individuals, families and communities in participatory learning and collaboration to nurture civic responsibility, leadership and effective social institutions. The programme supports collaborative training and development activities that strengthen the capacities of rural people and their institutions to improve agriculture and natural resource management practices; build assets; diversify income sources; and achieve food security, nutrition and health. The partners use a blend of science-based and indigenous knowledge to promote learning and capacity development.

The approach adopted by the programme utilizes community volunteers to assist in delivering adult education in several areas identified as critical to achieving food security. Volunteers are carefully screened by VEDCO. They are then trained to serve either as rural development extensionists or community nutrition and health workers. After initial training, the volunteers are expected to host regular educational meetings at their residence and to demonstrate improved crop and livestock management or nutrition and health practices. The volunteers are supported by subject matter specialists working for VEDCO who provide training materials, ongoing training and follow-up support. The community health and nutrition volunteers are identifiable in their blue jackets supplied by the programme. Community nutrition and health workers also receive basic equipment such as weighing scales, measuring boards, gloves, overcoats and bicycles.

Rural development extensionists receive shirts that identify their affiliation with the programme. They also receive basic extension equipment such as wheelbarrows, watering cans and bicycles. Rural development extensionists are supplied with improved planting materials (e.g. disease-free cassava cuttings and disease-free banana suckers) and improved crop varieties (e.g. orange flesh sweet potatoes and grain amaranth). They are also engaged in livestock distribution schemes involving pigs and poultry. They utilize these materials in demonstrations on their farms and distribute them to neighbours in conjunction with training on improved practices. Monitoring and evaluation support and training of subject matter specialists are provided by Iowa State University and Makerere University.

Volunteers take pride in their role in the community and in the results they have achieved. By mid 2007, 77 percent of the 800 households (approximately 7 500 people) working with the programme reported they had achieved food security, compared to 9 percent in early 2005.

CHALLENGE 6
Accommodating non-traditional learners

Non-traditional learners may include out of school youth (including girls and women), retired child soldiers, refugees and displaced persons, people in inaccessible and remote areas, disabled persons, ethnic minorities, working children, the elderly, nomads and pastoral communities, people suffering from diseases, and others. Each of these groups has a unique set of circumstances that make provision of educational services particularly challenging. In instances where non-traditional learners are also rural, the level of complexity in providing educational services tends to be high.

An overarching global goal is to reach these marginalized groups with adequate educational and training services to allow them to achieve a secure livelihood and to expand their options. The variety of educational needs of these groups means that there is a necessity for multiple educational safety nets to maximize participation rates in educational programmes. The importance of such programmes for rural youth and adults is underlined by the fact that over four out of five out of school children are rural (UNESCO, 2008) and therefore non-formal education represents the only opportunity to bridge their knowledge and skills gaps.

Functional adult literacy and non-formal basic education and training programmes provide a further learning chance to children, youth and adults who did not have the opportunity to pursue education in the formal systems of education. Such programmes can be coordinated with agriculture technical and vocational education and training centres and universities, as well as extension in the form of learning in context so that basic knowledge and competencies as well as technical and life skills are included in educational programmes.

In some cases, specially trained staff will be required to provide education and training services to non-traditional learners. Appreciation for cultural and ethnic diversity, language skills, and an understanding of the learners' background and challenges are critical to success in sustaining programmes that address learning needs of non-traditional populations. In the case of the hill tribes of northern Thailand, trained farmer volunteers have been effective at bridging the cultural divide (FAO, 2002a).

In some cases, additional resources will be needed to fund travel to remote areas such as mountain communities or small islands; to build residences for teachers assigned to areas where the target audience resides; to create safe and welcoming education facilities; and to provide special equipment, particularly in the case of disabled learners.

An example of an innovative approach to extending non-formal primary education to difficult to reach groups can be found in the experience of Orissa, India, whereby fisheries extension staff members were trained to provide these services to the children of fisherfolk. This pilot programme reached children from 6 to 14 years of age and prepared them to join formal school at a later date. In this programme, extension staff members who were already working with the parents of these children were tasked with also providing a service to the children, thereby taking advantage of the contacts they had already established to build confidence among their clientele (FAO, 2004b).

CHALLENGE (6)

An example from Thailand:
community involvement in curriculum determination for hill tribes

Organizations: Government of Thailand, local NGOs

Source: http://www.ftp://ftp.fao.org/docrep/fao/004/AC383E/AC383E00.pdf

Among the rural populations of Thailand, hill tribe people are among the most disadvantaged and vulnerable. While in recent years there have been some improvement in the socio-economic situation, modernization and influences from the lowlands have led to rapid changes in life patterns. Traditional self-sufficiency can no longer be maintained. Without skills and other means to cope, these communities suffer from deterioration in crucial areas such as agriculture, employment and socio-cultural values. Their production inputs are limited; they generally are denied access to basic social services, including education and health; and they lack opportunities for systematic skills development. Problems with citizenship and land settlement also complicate the life of hill tribe people.

Government policy towards the hill tribes is based on the Cabinet decision of 6 July 1976, which states that the government's intention is to integrate hill tribe people into the Thai State and give them full rights to practice their religions and maintain their cultures as "first class", self-reliant Thai citizens. The Royal Thai Government supports education for the hill tribe people through a four-way approach including: (1) participation and communication, (2) local curriculum development, (3) local capacity building and (4) inter-organization collaboration.

One response to this policy was the creation of the Hill Area Education Project in 1981 jointly implemented by the Departments of Public Welfare and Non-Formal Education responding to the needs and problems of hill tribe communities through a flexible low-cost community-based learning model. The programme combines the support of governmental and non-governmental organizations with community participation.

The educational approach is to reinforce and build on already existing knowledge and resources. To enhance a sense of ownership, various highland community learning centres were built by villagers using local materials and volunteer teachers came from the local community. Classes are conducted both for children and adults, based on a community-oriented curriculum which includes 35 percent of basic skills (including Thai language and mathematics) and 65 percent of life and social experience (19 basic topics/units and a completely open-ended local curriculum).

The curriculum is not graded. Completion of curricular objectives does not have to conform to fixed course duration. Children are required to spend around 6 000 hours to complete the entire community curriculum course and adults about 1 200 hours. Learning achievement is assessed by teachers along with villagers or officials according to different methods and criteria such as gender, age and ethnic group. To complement the learning at the centres, radio and satellite programmes are also offered. Self-study by community members is also encouraged.

An example from Kenya: non-traditional learning for children of pastoralist families
Organizations: GTZ (German Agency for Technical Cooperation), ActionAid Kenya

Source: http://www.care.org/careswork/whatwedo/education/docs/BGE_workthroughcommunities.pdf?source=170940420000&channel=REDGoogleTXT

With the assistance of NGOs, in particular ActionAid Kenya and the GTZ-assisted Samburu District Development Programme, and in response to a request from the community, a project was developed to help out of school Kenyan children from animal herding families obtain an education. For these poor rural families, children must help take care of and watch over the animals during the day. During dry seasons, children have to travel long distances to find pasture for their animals.

A non-formal education project was designed to accommodate the special needs of pastoralist children in Kenya. The *Lchekuti* (shepherds) project, planned and carried out in the Samburu District of Kenya, uses a multi-grade and multi-shift approach to learning. The project targets pastoralist children, both girls and boys, between the ages of 6 and 16. Generally, classes are held between 15.00 and 21.00 hours when the animals have been brought home from pasture. Another arrangement is to have two groups of students. One group of students attends class from Monday to Wednesday

65

while the other group stays with the animals. The group of young people taking care of the animals the first part of the week, then goes to class from Thursday to Saturday.

The curriculum is presented in Kiswahili and covers subjects such as numeracy, culture, religion, animal husbandry, business education and child care. The curriculum is determined by the local community, parents and students and is a reflection of the harsh environment of the Samburu District, a semi-arid region of Kenya.

In this non-formal educational setting, the learning is facilitated by volunteers and primary school teachers who have been trained and are supported by GTZ and ActionAid Kenya. Enrolment and attendance vary by season. During the wet season, when children do not have to go far to find good pasture, large numbers attend the classes. On the other hand, during the dry season, many children are not able to attend at all as they are out with animals looking for adequate grazing.

The factors leading to the relative success of this project include the need perceived by parents for some form of education for their out of school children and youth, and the involvement of the community in finding solutions to meeting this need. Another important contribution to success is the flexibility of timing and the short duration of classes allowing young people to continue their family herding responsibilities. The spirit of volunteerism and the willingness of volunteer teachers from the community are essential to the success of the project. The multi-grade system accommodates learners of different ages and learning ability. The multi-shift approach allows for needed flexibility in scheduling classes. It has also been found that the learning is gender-responsive and culturally appropriate which increases motivation of the students and support from parents and the community as a whole.

CHALLENGE 7
Redefining agricultural education

ERP includes agricultural education whose focus has been broadening to encompass a range of life and vocational skills related to both on-farm and off-farm employment. Historically, agricultural primary, secondary and technical and vocational education and training have focused sharply on preparing graduates for on-farm employment, whereas post-secondary and higher education have aimed to produce graduates to fill agriculturally related public sector positions (Avila *et al.*, 2005a). A generally prevailing universal assumption was that agriculture is the only economic activity viable in rural areas and, consequently, all agricultural education and training, at the primary, secondary and higher levels need to be production oriented.

To prepare individuals to succeed in increasingly knowledge-based rural economies linked to global supply chains, agricultural education will need to be redefined to reflect changes in rural areas. Agricultural education needs to respond to the changes in technology, emerging natural resource challenges, opportunities for on-farm and off-farm employment, the need to adapt to climate change, and opportunities in entrepreneurship and small enterprise development (Van Crowder *et al.*, 1998). The prevailing assumption needs to be broadened to include a range of income-generating activities operating in the rural space like agriculturally and non-agriculturally related enterprises. Developing rural people's resilience to adapt and to cope with a variety of global crises is critical to their ability to thrive. Crises may include those related to market fluctuations, climate change, drought as well as others. In extreme cases, a crisis might even lead national authorities to train rural people in skills needed in other locations. For example, the President of the Republic of Kiribati, a small island in South Pacific, indicated recently, as a way to cope with climate change and rising ocean levels, the need to "... train its people in skills that are needed in other lands and start emigrating. There is a shortage of nurses in Australia, so the women in Kiribati are trained to be nurses" (Greenway, 2009). China, on the other hand, might need to retrain rural migrants that cannot find work in cities, and are returning to rural areas. During the first five weeks of 2009, the

number of migrants returning to rural areas was roughly 20 millions, twice as many as estimated at the end of 2008, and a number that represents one in seven rural migrant workers (LaFraniere, 2009).

Incorporating agriculture into the primary school curriculum in rural areas seems quite logical from the perspective of food security. However, because of negative stereotypes associated with farming, such efforts can meet with resistance if they are viewed as focused only on preparing students to be farmers. Schools that have integrated agriculture into science and/or business curricula and those that use school gardening as an experiential learning laboratory have had greater success. Additionally, incorporating health and nutrition into the curriculum helps students appreciate the systemic relationships within food, agriculture and health (FAO/UNESCO-IIEP, 2004a).

At colleges and institutes that offer technical and vocational agricultural education for preparing technicians to work in the private sector and government service, there is a need to broaden and update curricula to include a number of new topics related to sustainable rural development. These curricula might include sustainable agriculture approaches, social change processes especially for those planning to work in extension and with NGOs, and a better understanding of emerging challenges such as climate change, variability in agricultural input and product costs, and the impacts (and opportunities) associated with participation in global supply chains.

Higher agricultural education has a role to play in supporting education and training in the rural context. The engaged university is one that seeks out opportunities to work directly with communities. In the late 1990s, the Escuela Agrícola Panamericana (Zamorano), an international institution located in Honduras, carried out an ambitious multifaceted transformation programme on the evolving needs of the college's external constituencies and society at large (FAO/UNESCO-IIEP, 2004b). EARTH University in Costa Rica has developed a strong link to surrounding communities with benefits accruing to both the communities

and the students from EARTH who interact with them (http://www.earth.ac.cr/ing/index.php). In so doing, the community and the university are both strengthened. Universities gain first-hand knowledge of the challenges currently confronting rural people and can better address these specific challenges through research and teaching. Universities can play a key role in training teachers and extension staff, in assisting with the development of curriculum, in developing new technologies of relevance to rural people, in leading agricultural innovation systems, and helping with monitoring and evaluation of educational rural programmes (FAO/UNESCO-IIEP, 2007a). Over the past several decades, Chinese higher agricultural education institutions have been producing highly qualified graduates for agricultural research, extension services and rural administration. The institutional reform, initiated in the 1990s, introduced into the curriculum courses relevant to rural people's needs such as 'human resource development for rural development', 'gender and development', 'participatory training methodologies', and 'participatory community development'. Students graduated under this curriculum play an active role in addressing current local and global challenges to rural development and livelihoods (FAO/UNESCO-IIEP, 2004c).

CHALLENGE ⑦

An example from Kyrgyzstan:
adapting vocational agricultural education to the new market economy

Organizations: Helvetas, Ministry of Labour and Social Protection, GTZ, UNDP, Agriculture Universities of Naryn and Bishkek, Swiss College of Agriculture in Zollikofen, Switzerland

Source: http://www.helvetas.org/global/pdf/projects/asien/04_09_berufsbildung_e.pdf

Following the collapse of the Soviet Union, agriculture changed from a state-owned enterprise to private ownership. In Kyrgyzstan, rural people who had been engaged in agriculture generally had experience in very specialized areas of production. With the change to a market economy, rural people had to take on the role of independent farmers, responsible for all aspects of working the land and marketing their produce.

Since 2001, Helvetas, a non-profit private development organization based in Switzerland, has been working with other partners to develop advisory services for farmers. They soon realized that there was a need for more in-depth training in agriculture to help farmers meet the demands of the new economy. The Agricultural and Rural Vocational Education project was established in Naryn oblast to help people living in the rural areas of this poor region of the country develop knowledge, skills and attitudes to manage private farms and other rural-based businesses.

The project created a new form of vocational agricultural education for men and women farmers in seven pilot partner schools. The learning is based on the situation and conditions associated with farming in this region of Kyrgyzstan. The curriculum was developed using a participatory approach involving farmers, students, parents, teachers, school administrators as well as local and national agriculture specialists.

The project started with 100 students in two schools in the villages of Kochkor and Ottuk, but soon expanded to include over 650 students covering the entire Naryn oblast. The national methodological centre of the Ministry of Labour and Social Protection has been involved in the project so that the vocational agricultural education programme could be applied to other regions of the country.

The vocational agricultural education programme involves three levels of education, progressing from the category of "farm labourer" to "master farmer". The first level is for a total of one and a half year of education and provides basic skills training to carry out general farming tasks. The next level is "farmer" where young men and women graduate after three years and are fully able to operate a farm on their own. The next level, "master farmer", takes the training one step further and focuses on market-oriented entrepreneurship. Graduates who obtain this level of training are also qualified to provide practical field training to other farmers.

Initially students, as part of an apprenticeship system, spend one third of their education time working on host farms. The training involves both theory and practical experience on the school farms. Students are encouraged throughout the training to acquire a business-oriented and problem-solving approach, which is new for many teachers. Teachers also have to learn new roles as fellow learners, coaches and facilitators of the learning process. School managers learn to administer the new educational system and continually look for ways to strengthen and improve existing systems and structures within their institutions.

An example from Paraguay:
agricultural education: teaching children from low-income rural areas how to save, invest and earn money

Organization: Fundación Paraguaya

Source: http://www.fundacionparaguaya.org.py/index.php?c=208 and http://www.theworldchallenge.co.uk/html/home.html

Paraguay has a large rural population and is one of the poorest countries in Latin America where two thirds of the land is held by 2 percent of the population. The majority are peasant farmers on small land holdings. It is a country where the wealthy stay wealthy and the poor tend to remain poor. In 2002, Martin Burt, the former mayor of Asunción, with the assistance of the Fundación Paraguaya for cooperation and development, set up *Escuela Agricola* to help children from the poorest families in the countryside become rural entrepreneurs.

Escuela Agricola is one of the 12 projects in the world that have been nominated for the World Challenge 2008 Award, sponsored by BBC, Newsweek and the Shell

CHALLENGE (7)

Corporation recognizing projects and small businesses from around the world that have shown enterprise and innovation at the grassroots level. In 2007, the school hosted the World Conference on Self-Sufficient Agricultural Schools with representatives attending from 22 countries in Africa, Asia, Latin America, the United States of America and the United Kingdom.

The school was converted from a highly subsidized standard agricultural high school to a self-sufficient and fully organic farm school for children of poor rural families. The school has 62 hectares of land and approximately 7 000 square metres of fairly modern buildings. Students spend half of their time outside of the classroom where they learn not only how to increase yields but also how to maximize profits and sell their produce.

Escuela Agricola teaches students how to make the most of their parent's land using the latest in organic technology. In addition to agriculture and other basic academic subjects, the school teaches life skills and reproductive health. The school is completely self-sufficient. Students grow most of their own food and sell value-added products such as cheese and yoghurts. The school even runs a small income-earning hotel, where urban people can come to enjoy the countryside and learn a little about agriculture. Most importantly, the people from the city who visit the school farm and stay at the hotel see the students not as poor peasant farm youth, but rather as a group of young, highly motivated and technically skilled entrepreneurs.

Students, both boys and girls, come from very poor rural families who generally have many children and no hope of providing them possibilities of an advanced education. *Escuela Agricola* provides room and board, as most students come from remote areas far from urban centres. Students, who come from most of the departments in the country, must have completed grade 9 and be between 15 and 21 years of age. Their families have to own some land where the students can go back and be expected to develop a profitable agribusiness. Students who graduate from the *Escuela Agricola* benefit from the Fundación Paraguaya's microenterprise development programme, which allows the Central Bank of Paraguay to lend money to the young poor farmers.

CHALLENGE 8
Skills training for rural people

Despite the existence of thousands of agriculture and rural development technical and vocational education training (TVET) institutions and skills training courses all over the world, the international community has placed little political priority, very few financial resources, and only minor research attention on this subsector. The UNESCO policy studies and recommendations published in recent years on TVET focus mainly on urban dwellers needs and institutions. Since the late 1980s and for about 20 years, the World Bank has underestimated the importance of TVET in general. However, with the World Bank's recent shift to prioritization of agriculture (World Bank, 2007c) as a key development issue, the importance of agricultural education and training was rediscovered and is now being promoted as a crucial pro-poor investment (World Bank, 2007a).

A narrow skills base can limit employment options and reduce livelihood alternatives for rural citizens. Skills training in rural areas needs to include a balance among life skills, food production skills and self-employment skills. Appropriate non-formal skills training for adults and school drop-outs can permit rural people to diversify their skills for a more secure livelihood and greater resilience during times of stress (FAO/UNESCO-IIEP, 2006b). Vocational and technical education and training could benefit from the inclusion of agriculture and rural development content to ensure relevance of the programmes (Avila *et al.*, 2005ab). Leaders from African countries emphasized the need for non-formal livelihood skills training for adults and school drop-outs aimed at income-generating activities through self-employment (FAO/UNESCO-IIEP, 2006b).

Innovative models have been developed in Lao People's Democratic Republic, where production-based vocational schools combine learning, earning and doing (FAO/ UNESCO-IIEP, 2002). Another example is the Junior Farmer Field and Life School programme

77

in Mozambique that deals with agricultural as well as life skills development among young rural citizens (FAO/UNESCO-IIEP, 2006b). The FAO Interdepartmental Working Group on Training for Technicians and Capacity Building has identified five examples of "best practices" and these were published in booklet form (FAO, 2007a).

In some instances, there is a tremendous urgency to this task. For example, many youth in rural areas can no longer be thought of as "future farmers"; they are today's farmers because of the loss of parents to HIV/AIDS. The traditional apprenticeship within the family economy has been lost and, with it, also invaluable indigenous knowledge. Vocational and technical education and training programmes for children and youth are one response to this problem. The Junior Farmer Field Schools undertaken with orphans of HIV/AIDS parents are running in several African countries with FAO technical assistance.

An example from Nigeria:
university outreach delivers seminar to local farmers

Organizations: Teach a Man to Fish, Akwamfon Sustainable Agricultural and Community Education Initiative and the Akwa Ibom Agricultural Development Programme

Source: http://www.teachamantofish.org.uk/blogs/ASCA/2008/04/sife-akadep-aid-rural-agriculture.html

The student organization, Students in Free Enterprise (SIFE), from the University of Uyo in Nigeria, in collaboration with the Akwa Ibom Agricultural Development Programme (AKADEP) and the Akwamfon Sustainable Agricultural and Community Education Initiative planned and carried out a seminar for men, women and youth from the Ikpe Annang Community and five surrounding villages. The theme of the seminar was Agriculture as a Business. Crop and livestock experts from AKADEP spoke on various topics while a representative from the SIFE moderated the seminar.

Topics discussed included how to profit by using good farm practices such as the timing of farming operations to maximize production and take advantage of market demand; the use of improved types and breeds of livestock; and the use of a combination of organic and inorganic fertilizers to maximize production and be most environmentally responsible.

On the animal husbandry side, a presentation was made on the potential for the production of grasscutters to increase farm income and food security. Grasscutters, a small rodent, are appreciated as food by many African households and bring a good price in the market. As a type of bushmeat, the animals are usually hunted; however, with proper care, they can be raised on the farm. They are very productive, breed during all the year, have many offspring and grow fast. Farmers were also told how to acquire lime to control the acidity of their soils. Other useful advice included how to order improved crop varieties and good quality livestock, as well as advice on dry season farming of fluted pumpkins and other vegetable crops that are very much in demand during the dry season and have a good market value.

Farmers raised many questions during the seminar. In the follow-up plan of action, it was agreed that SIFE students and advisors would return to the village to demonstrate good crop and livestock production practices according to the needs and interests of the farmers. It was also agreed that the farmers would register with AKADEP so that the local farmers' association could be linked with major markets to sell their produce and livestock.

Some farmers mentioned that this was the first time that the government had presented such a programme in their village. The farmers were appreciative of the seminar and said that otherwise they would have had to spend much money and travel long distances to get the kind of information that was provided.

An example from Kenya:
building capacity of goat farmers through skills training

Organizations: FARM Africa, local governments and Meru Goat Breeders Association

Source: http://www.farmafrica.org.uk/programme.cfm?programmeid=30&context=subject&subjectid=3 and www.ilri.org/johnvercoeconference/files/

Presentations/01_ChristiePeacock_Farm%20Africa%20case%20study.pps

Small farmers in Kenya face many problems like limited potential for increases in crop yields; land holdings shrinking because of fragmentation; cash crop prices that are stagnant or are falling; and unreliable support services for cattle. Based on the lessons learned from an earlier project, the Meru Dairy Goat and Healthcare Project, which was carried out from 1996 to 2004 in central Kenya, a new dairy goat improvement project was started in the semi-arid areas of Kitui and Mwingi Districts in Eastern Kenya to increase farm incomes and household food security.

The project is based on the premise that any real significant increase in animal production in Kenya will come through a breed improvement programme coupled with good quality animal health care services. Under the project, farmers obtain up to three litres of milk per day per animal using the Toggenburg crosses compared to the 200 ml generally obtained from local goat breeds. Each village group received a purebred Toggenburg buck for cross breeding, along with four does for a breeding unit to maintain purebred animals and ensure a sustainable supply of pure breeding stock for replacement and expansion to other areas.

The project is unique as it is a totally community-based dairy goat production and breed improvement programme, supported by a private veterinary system, local extension services and a farmer-managed breeders association to take care of breeding arrangements and manage all inputs. All this has been possible through community organization and skills training to build the capacity of milk goat producers and local technicians. The village dairy farmer groups are 21 with over 500 members and almost 70 percent of the members are women.

An initial three-day training programme for the farmers was provided to enhance group cohesiveness, develop a shared vision of the functioning of the local dairy goat breeding and production programme and give a chance to members to share experiences and lessons learned. Additional training included such topics as group dynamics to strengthen group decision-making and action; goat breeding techniques; how to provide for adequate housing, goat identification and record keeping; feed conversion; and kid rearing. There was also training to help selected farmers set up and maintain a village breeding station.

As part of the capacity building for local support services, community extension workers and village drug shop attendants were trained. Extension workers received training on animal husbandry practices, group dynamics and farmer-to-farmer extension skills. One week of training was provided to nine drug shop attendants where they received orientation as to their role in the decentralized community animal health system and the principles under which it operates. To further develop their capacity, the drug shop attendants were trained on effective communication with clients; how to improve on drug shops public image; common animal diseases and their clinical signs; and the drugs that are used to treat various diseases.

CHALLENGE 9
Recruitment and retention of extension and school staff

Having talented and committed extension staff and teachers posted in rural areas is central to the success of educational enterprises at all levels. Preparing sufficient numbers of qualified and motivated extension staff and teachers is a critical initial step. However, it is far from automatic that these individuals will gravitate towards rural postings upon graduation. Recruitment for and retention in rural areas present significant challenges and require special attention. Rural teachers are difficult to recruit and retain because of factors such as a lower social status than urban teachers, feelings of isolation, distance from family and friends, lack of carrier development and training opportunities, lack of incentives, difficulty adjusting to rural lifestyles, lack of amenities, difficulty of communication, poor shopping, and others.

One innovation identified by ERP partners is the reform of recruitment practices by attracting prospective extension workers and teachers who are originally from rural areas. Teachers who work where they grew up are more likely to stay. Some efforts have also been made to "grow your own" teachers by encouraging (and subsidizing) rural youth to consider teaching professions. *Ad hoc* colleges to train rural teachers are part of the Rural Education Programme running in Colombia.

Another area identified as ripe for change is the deployment policies that can be adjusted to make rural areas more attractive. This can be done through bonuses, higher salaries compared to other government employees in rural areas, loan forgiveness, provision of subsidized housing, access to better health care, posting newly qualified teachers/extension workers in pairs, establishment of career progression options, and other similar policies.

In Malaysia, for example, a package of incentives, including a piece of land and training in agriculture, was used to encourage teachers to stay in rural areas. In Lao People's Democratic Republic, profit sharing in school-based income-generating activities is allowed whereby both students and teachers benefit financially (FAO/UNESCO/ IIEP, 2002). Another way to keep teachers and extension staff connected is to provide, where feasible, mobile phones and Internet service for staff based in remote areas.

CHALLENGE (9)

Yet, even with the implementation of these and other innovative ideas, there will likely still be shortages of staff in rural areas in some countries. Adjustments will need to be made. For example, increased mobility of a smaller number of extension staff in rural areas can expand coverage if adequate funds for transport are available. In the formal education sector, multi-grade classrooms are one response to teacher shortages (UNESCO-IIEP, 2003).

An example from Peru:
Kamayoq: village farmer-to-farmer extension workers promote farmer innovation and experimentation in rural areas
Organization: Practical Action

Source: http://pdf.usaid.gov/pdf_docs/PNADF052.pdf and http://www.aprendesperu.org/

As in other countries, structural adjustments in the 1990s led to the breakdown of traditional agricultural research and extension services in Peru. The existing government system was weak, focusing primarily on technology transfer and ignoring farmer innovation and experimentation. By 1992, the government extension programme run by the National Institute for Agricultural Research had fewer than 100 officers for the entire country. The assumption was that extension services for all farmers would be provided by the private sector. What happened in the field is that resource-poor farmers were not able to pay for these services mostly directed to larger commercial operations.

Practical Action, an NGO working in the Quechua-speaking farming communities of the Peruvian Andes helped villagers solve the problem by developing their capacity through education and training for a sustainable farmer-to-farmer extension system supporting farmer innovation and experimentation. Based on the pedagogic approach of the Brazilian educator, Paulo Freire, Practical Action designed a training approach that respected the social and cultural context of the local farmers and placed an emphasis on learn-by-doing and farmer participation.

Practical Action's work began on irrigation technologies in the early 1990s, using farmer extension agents called *Kamayoq*. *Kamayoq* is a word from the Inca Empire language that meant a respected group of people who could predict climate and weather and

made recommendations for sowing and other agricultural practices. The use of the term *Kamayoq* is significant in that it is a direct link to the Quechua people's historic past.

By the mid-1990s, Practical Action realized that the activities had to be broader than irrigation to better meet the needs of farmers. In 1996, as a result of considerable donor funding, a *Kamayoq* school was established in Sicuani, about 140 kilometres from Cuzco. The school has been operating ever since and has the fundamental objective of training groups of farmers who are then responsible to go back to their communities to train other farmers.

A key to the training is to encourage the *Kamayoq* to be creative with farmers and encourage innovation and experimentation to deal with agricultural and veterinary problems. As farming conditions in the Andes are very complex, there are no standardized solutions. The training courses take place over an eight-month period, which include approximately 27 training sessions. Over 200 *Kamayoq* have been trained so far and of

CHALLENGE ⑨

these, 15 percent were women. At the school, some of the training takes place in the classroom, but most is carried out at the various field locations.

There have been many positive impacts from this programme. Before the *Kamayoq* started their work, most families were subsistence farmers. Now they grow subsistence crops but also, particularly among women, they raise onions and carrots for the market. Families have been able to increase income from market sales and thus pay for education for their children. The rates of mortality among cattle have fallen greatly as farmers are now better able to detect animal disease and take action to prevent losses.

An example from Mozambique:
teacher training college helps farmers to increase production through Farmer Club project

Organizations: Humana People to People, USDA, Plant Aid Inc., Government of Mozambique

Source: http://www.humana.org/dns/Articel.asp?NewsID=35

Since 1993, Humana People to People has worked to develop teacher training colleges in Mozambique, Angola and Malawi. In that year, the first teacher training college was opened in Maputo with support from the Development Aid from People to People in Mozambique. The college was strongly inspired by the Necessary Teacher Training College model from Tvind in Denmark. There are now six teacher training colleges in Mozambique.

One of the Teacher Training Colleges in Chimoio Province is working with local villages of communal farmers to foster increased agricultural production in order to strengthen food security and increase household incomes. The work is carried out around the formation of community Farmer Clubs. The college has organized ten Farmer Clubs in Macossa, Barue, Sussundenga, Chimoio, Gondola and Manica Districts in Chimoio Province.

The clubs are run by graduate teachers and students in their 11-month teaching practice who will be working in rural primary schools throughout the country. Each Farmer Club has from 30 to 55 members. The teachers are responsible for providing relevant lessons related to agricultural production and marketing, carrying out practical demonstrations in the field, and providing other types of overall assistance to the communal farmer members.

The student teachers are assigned to rural primary schools in the Province. They are given bicycles in order to reach all farmer members of each Farmer Club in the area of operation. Farmer Club members receive training through the presentation of 15-18 courses, depending on their interests and needs. The courses include some theory with demonstrations and practical work carried out on Saturdays. Most demonstration plots are located at the village primary schools where student teachers have been assigned. In addition to the courses and field demonstration work, student teachers are on-call to help individual farmer members of the Farmer Group at any time.

Student teachers also help members of the Farmer Club market their produce. Some farmers provide vegetables for use in the school and other produce is sold at the local market. Harvests from the demonstration plots are donated to schools, orphanages and prisons. The project has been very successful in helping communal farmers and members of the village Farmer Clubs gain the necessary skills and knowledge to enable them to improve their agricultural production and marketing, and thus increase overall household incomes and strengthen food security.

CHALLENGE 9

CHALLENGE 10
Effective pro-rural policies

In the absence of adequate pro-rural policies on education and financing, many of the innovations mentioned in previous sections will not be feasible. However, motivating major changes in policy and resource allocation to favour rural citizens is generally very difficult to achieve, owing to the absence of powerful political forces that advocate for rural people.

National policies and strategies that effectively address ERP recognize and target the diversity of needs of rural people such as agro-ecological differences, geographical differences, and socio-economic and cultural differences (FAO/UNESCO/IIEP, 2006a). However national investments in ERP are seldom a top priority. But, as Burchi and De Muro (2007) found, education is a neglected key to food security. They indicated that "... the association between food insecurity and primary education is very high" (p. 3) and also that "... *primary* more than basic, secondary or tertiary education for rural

people contributes to the promotion of food security in rural areas" *(ibid.,* p. 38). Because of the link between education and food security, education was shown to be an area worthy of further investment. "... primary education is a crucial element to reduce food insecurity in rural areas, even when compared to other factors such as access to water, health and sanitation" *(ibid.,* p. 3).

In general, ERP partners believe there has been an under-investment in developing rural people's capacities by the state. Basic education is generally considered a public good, and most believe it should be funded by the state. It can be argued, likewise, that rural extension is also a public good when it is dealing with food security for the most vulnerable populations. Poor farmers generally cannot afford to pay for school fees for their children nor for advice on food security interventions, and they generally will not pay for extension advice on environmental improvements. Therefore, public investment is often required to address these audiences.

Responsive, pro-rural policies cannot be developed without an adequate information base. Data on ERP that enable governments and the international community to

89

understand the precise educational needs of rural people will aid in the development of effective national policies and will help the donor community understand why ERP should be repositioned higher on the world agenda.

National governments are finding it challenging to build effective ERP programmes in the face of decreasing donor investment in education, training and rural development (FAO, 2002c). But the argument for making such investments is compelling. Burchi and De Muro (2007) stated that "if a developing country such as Mali, which is among those with lowest levels of education, manages to double access to primary education, it can reduce the intensity of food insecurity by approximately 20 or 24 percent in rural areas" (p. 38). They concluded that education for rural people, which is the main group of people directly involved in food production, processing, and commercialisation, "is a key factor in fighting food insecurity in developing countries" (ibid., p. 37). In this example, an investment in one sector can have a multiplier effect resulting in a positive impact on another sector.

An example from Peru:
innovations in decentralization improve quality of education for rural people

Organizations: USAID, Academy for Educational Development, Government of Peru, AprenDes

Source: http://pdf.usaid.gov/pdf_docs/PNADF052.pdf and http://www.aprendesperu.org/

The project, Innovations in Decentralization and Active Schools (AprenDes), in rural Peru has accomplished a great deal since it started in 2003. With a partnership between USAID/Peru and the Ministry of Education, the project is being carried out in schools and school communities in rural areas of the San Martin region of Peru. The project supports the Peruvian Government's 2003 Education Law, which promotes decentralization as a way to improve the quality of education in the country. The project is implemented by the Academy for Educational Development and focuses on decentralized local management of schools, improved educational quality and democratic practices. The goal of this project is to improve the quality of ERP from bottom up as well as top down.

The project focuses on the design of effective decentralization policies and their implementation through community level management of quality education in the regional and local context. Community members and students themselves become involved as the project promotes group work, self-initiated learning, democratic behaviour and parent involvement. In this way, students become active participants in the social and economic life of their local communities. AprenDes in San Martin region has already impacted over 6 000 students in 140 one-teacher and multi-grade rural schools. The project works to strengthen the capacity of the Ministry of Education, local governments and others to help them assume appropriate and supportive roles in the decentralization process. The teacher's role is to facilitate the learning process. Project facilitators are hired to train the teachers, give them technical support and promote the development of effective learning materials.

Under the national Decentralization Law, each local school is managed by an Educational Council, made up of representatives of students, parents, school directors and community leaders. The local Educational Councils receive training and then work together to develop the annual school plan. The schools under the project are converted from traditional schools to "active schools", characterized by active learning and by the participation of parents, students, teachers, members of the community and school administrators. In a traditional school, the teacher lectures and the students try to commit the material to memory by copying notes from the blackboard. In the active schools, students work in small groups and learn reading, mathematics and natural sciences in learning centres. Students research and analyze real problems in the community. They are involved in community service projects and are actively involved in the management of their school. Students prepare oral stories and write articles about life and work in their community.

In the active schools, teachers become facilitators of learning. They facilitate learning in small groups. Networks of teachers meet periodically to share experiences, observe other classes and solve educational problems. Teachers learn new techniques through practical experience, training and feedback from other teachers and are responsible for developing their own learning materials. They design training manuals and adapt learning guides based on the local conditions and prepare materials important to the needs of their students.

CHALLENGE 10

An example from El Salvador:
EDUCO - reform expands educational opportunities for children in the poorest rural communities

Organizations: Ministry of Education, World Bank, UNESCO, UNDP

Source: http://www.ifc.org/ifcext/edinvest.nsf/Content/EvaluationStudies; http://www.iadb.org/ethics/documentos/lie_impl-i.pdf; and http://siteresources.worldbank.org/EDUCATION/Resources/278200-1099079877269/547664-1099079934475/547667-1135281552767/ElSalvador_EDUCO.pdf

As late as the early 1990s, El Salvador had one of the weakest educational systems in all of Latin America, with high levels of repetition and drop-out. The 12-year long civil war in the 1980s contributed to a weak education system, especially in rural areas. Some schools, particularly in the north (Chalatenango, Morazán and Cabanas) and San Vicente, in the central region, were closed definitely because of the frequent army and guerrilla confrontations. Existing rural schools supported by the government were of such poor quality that parents thought school was a waste of time and many kept their children, especially girls, at home to take care of younger siblings and do household chores. In 1990, the net enrolment rate for primary education was 61.3 percent meaning that more than half million primary-age children were not in school.

In 1991, with the support of the World Bank and the Inter-American Development Bank, the Ministry of Education established the Community Participation Education Programme to expand educational opportunities by providing pre-primary and primary education to the poorest communities in El Salvador. The Spanish acronym of the programme is EDUCO. The programme started with 8 416 students in 263 schools. By 1996, the programme was expanded to include 168 672 students in 5 721 schools. The objectives of the programme are to increase access to education for the poorest rural communities; promote local community participation in education; and improve the quality of pre-school and primary education.

Under this decentralized educational reform, parents in a community elect among themselves a managing body called the Community Education Association (ACE). The Ministry of Education enters into a renewable one-year contract, which is governed by a formal outline of rights and responsibilities between the government and the community. The community agrees to deliver a given curriculum to a determined number of students. The ACEs are the direct employer of the teachers. They select, hire and dismiss those teachers who do not perform up to a certain standard. Teachers' performance and attendance are monitored by the ACE. The community associations are also responsible for equipping and maintaining the school facilities. To function, each ACE receives a direct transfer of funds from the Ministry of Education.

Evaluations of EDUCO indicate that the programme is in fact serving the poorest communities in El Salvador. There are no differences in academic performance between students attending the EDUCO schools and those going to traditional schools, even though the socio-economic conditions of the EDUCO students are inferior to those attending traditional schools. The EDUCO schools generally have worse infrastructure and basic services than the traditional schools and yet the EDUCO schools tend to have more and better teaching materials. Most importantly, parents of EDUCO students are more involved in the education of their children.

THE ERP PARTNERSHIP

fter six years from inception, the ERP partnership is composed of a group of approximately 350 members committed to fostering ERP. ERP members represent the national and international public sectors including international organizations and governments, as well as media, academia, business sector and civil society like NGOs, farmers, youth and women organizations. Several volunteers have graciously supported the ERP Coordination Unit and the attendees of the ERP capacity development and other initiatives have provided invaluable inputs to shaping the ERP policy and knowledge. ERP utilized these partnerships to promote capacity development and the exchange of good practices as well as policy dialogue on ERP with member countries and international organizations and to promote cooperation among ministries of education and ministries of agriculture, donors and with the civil society. FAO has provided the physical, financial and technical resources to host the ERP Coordination Unit at FAO headquarters since 2002.

ERP PARTNERSHIP RESOURCES

Activities under this programme have been mainly funded by FAO regular programme and through financial support to FAO by the Italian Agency for Development Cooperation (DGCS), the Republic of San Marino, the French Ministry of Foreign and European Affairs, and the World Food Programme (WFP). Additional support through non-cash resources was provided by UNESCO headquarters and UNESCO-IIEP through staff time as well as from other UNESCO units, notably the UNESCO regional offices in Bangkok and Santiago and the UNESCO office in Beijing.

The French Agency for Development in the framework of the *Appui au développement de l'expertise en formation agricole et rurale* (AdexFAR) project, the French Ministry of Agriculture and Fisheries, the Association for the Development of Education in Africa (ADEA), the Inter-American Institute for Cooperation on Agriculture (IICA), the Global Development Learning Network (GDLN) of the World Bank, the European Commission, the Consultative Group on International Agricultural Research (CGIAR), the Farmers of the Future initiative of the World Agroforestry Centre (ICRAF), the Global Forum

on Agricultural Research (GFAR) and a network of NGOs from the North and the South as well as the US-based Iowa State University and some Italian, Colombian and British universities also contributed mobilizing cash and non-cash resources needed for the implementation of the ERP partnership activities. In addition, all members contributed through their involvement in ERP activities since this is the main condition for membership. The NGOs' contribution in fostering ERP at national and international levels has been and is very significant given that they are a key stakeholder in promoting field work with rural people. Hereafter follows a description of ERP activities.

RESEARCH AND KNOWLEDGE MANAGEMENT AND SHARING

ERP started with an in-depth global study revisiting the interaction among education, agriculture, food security and rural development, jointly conducted by FAO and UNESCO-IIEP and an assessment of the state of public policies on ERP and the concepts that inspire them. During this phase, interaction between specialized institutions was promoted, relevant data collected and analyzed, and findings from the study published in the book *Education for rural development: towards new policy responses*, which sets the policy framework for the ERP initiative (FAO/UNESCO-IIEP, 2003). The partnership expanded its research to the contribution of higher tertiary agricultural education to enhancing rural people's lives by publishing four case studies (FAO/UNESCO-IIEP, 2004b; FAO/UNESCO-IIEP, 2004c; FAO/UNESCO-IIEP, 2005c; FAO/UNESCO-IIEP, 2005d). Collaboration with EARTH University, with the Sustainability, Education and the Management of Change in the Tropics (SEMCIT) seminar series and with Iowa State University, as well as specific capacity development workshops called by FAO and UNESCO on this topic were undertaken.

All these activities ensured that ERP would be developed according to a solid research base. A global repository of the knowledge base of ERP has been established at FAO and is accessible worldwide via the Internet (http://www.fao.org/sd/erp/) in five languages. An ERP Series, available in hard copy as well as online, has been publishing further ERP research and allowing the sharing of new knowledge and good practices. The DVD and online publication of the ERP Tool Kit with teaching and learning materials for formal and non-formal agricultural education and other subjects relevant to rural people's lives, for teachers and instructors, farmers, extension personnel and the general public (http://www.fao.org/sd/erp/ERPtktoolkit_en.htm) is an example of the focus placed on producing and sharing training materials to strengthen national capacity to promote ERP at country, regional and international levels.

POLICY DIALOGUE AND CAPACITY DEVELOPMENT

Through seven regional and three donors capacity development workshops, the partnership examined how the EFA National Action Plans as well as the Rural Development Plans were focusing attention on the educational needs of rural people. The regional workshops focused on ERP in Asia (FAO/UNESCO-IIEP, 2002; FAO/UNESCO-IIEP, 2006a), Latin America (FAO/UNESCO-IIEP, 2004b), Africa (FAO/UNESCO-IIEP, 2006b; FAO, 2007a) and the Caribbean (FAO/UNESCO-IIEP, 2006c) targeting decision-makers from the ministries of agriculture and education as well as civil society, international organizations and academia.

Through such activities, education policy makers and planners learned from agriculture and rural development staff involved in non-formal skills training and extension, and in technical and vocational and higher agricultural education. Extension, frequently marginalized by the rigidity of a single sector approach where formal and non-formal education are addressed as separate realities, benefited from the exchange of practices with other delivery modalities. National case studies on ERP were produced as part of the preparation of the seven regional workshops and studies on Eastern

Europe countries, such as Bosnia and Herzegovina, Croatia, Serbia and Kosovo, were also produced under FAO normative programme. These and other activities are reported in http://www.fao.org/sd/erp/ERPotheractivities_en.htm.

Overall, good progress has been made in mainstreaming ERP in the international policy agenda. ERP is included in a number of key policy statements like, for example, the Report by the Secretary-General on the work of the Organization to the fifty-ninth session of the General Assembly (UN, 2004) on achieving the universal primary education goal of the United Nations Millennium Declaration. ERP was discussed at national and international policy forums such as the 2005 EFA High-Level Group Meeting held in Beijing, where ERP was identified as a strategic global policy priority for the coming years. The ADEA 2008 Biennale and the International Conference on Education (Geneva, 2008), the World Conference on Education for Sustainable Development (Bonn, 2009) have focused on equity in education and training and addressed the urban-rural education gap as key challenges to the achievement of the MDGs. Several other international events or policy documents acknowledging ERP importance are reported in the ERP site http://www.fao.org/sd/erp/ERPUNdocuments_en.htm.

ERP worked through its partners simultaneously at the policy, capacity building and grassroots levels. Both normative and field works were undertaken. Emphasis was on the policy level to ensure the greatest impact, cost-effectiveness and a multiplier effect (FAO/ UNESCO-IIEP, 2005a). Other examples include the Kosovo Strategy for ERP (MEST/MAFRD/FAO, 2004) and the preparation of guidelines for planning and monitoring ERP implementation (FAO/ UNESCO-IIEP, 2007b). The online tool kit responds to the need for competencies and basic skills that are in demand among rural people, such as management of crops and forests; soil and water management; land rights; issues related to animals and pastoralism; biodiversity, rural finance, agribusiness and marketing; book-keeping; fishery; food and nutrition; as well as other aspects important to sustainable livelihoods such as planning ERP, HIV/ AIDS, gender, peace education and training for conflict management, and communication. The ERP Tool Kit is constantly updated through member's inputs and is available at http://www.fao.org/sd/erp/ERPtktoolkit_en.htm. The impact of the ERP partnership on the media is documented in http://www.fao.org/sd/erp/ERParticlesPresslast_en.htm.

REASONS FOR SUCCESS

The magnitude of the endeavour to promote ERP cannot be addressed by any single organization or institution. The success of the ERP global initiative is attributed, among other reasons, to the following:

>> partnerships forged have expedited and facilitated implementation;

>> a strong partnership between FAO and UNESCO including active participation of Field Offices from both organizations;

>> successful alliances and collaboration among ministries of agriculture and education, NGOs, international organizations and academic and research institutions and the media in developing countries and at international level;

>> a holistic approach linking normative and pilot field work which facilitates the development of a sound foundation (theory) to move forward the partnership initiative;

>> the strategic choice to focus the ERP programme on upstream policy and capacity development which ensures cost-effectiveness and a multiplier effect;

>> the informal management style that allowed great freedom to explore ideas and build new relations and to operate at a very low cost; and

>> permanent monitoring of the validity of our commitments – FAO's as well as those of partners.

THE ERP PARTNERSHIP WAY FORWARD

Educating all rural people is a huge challenge, and much is still to be done considering the number of illiterate adults and out of school children living in rural areas. The policy work being well established, it is now appropriate to shift to a phase whereby resources will be focused on implementation at country level. During this next phase, new investments will be needed at the national level. FAO, as a knowledge-based organization, will continue to collect, analyze, interpret and disseminate the knowledge required for the world to meet the food and nutrition needs of all its citizens and to provide global governance "with respect to ... the improvement of education and administration relating to nutrition, food and agriculture, and the spread of public knowledge of nutritional and agricultural science and practice" (FAO, 1945). UNESCO and the World Bank are uniquely suited to facilitating ERP implementation at the national level given that this role lies within their mandates to support the advancement of education at such a level. EFA National plans, the Fast Track Initiative, poverty reduction strategies and National Rural Development Plans as well as the One UN initiative can yield significant results as the lessons from the ERP first phase are implemented. UNESCO's leadership and technical support to ERP at the country level during this next phase would need to be strengthened. FAO is in a good position to contribute as a supporting entity to the work of UNESCO in the specific areas of FAO expertise.

At the national level, the hallmark of the ERP implementation will be a systemic needs-based approach that fosters education (including extension) by expanding access and improving quality for all children, youth and adults. This can be done only by strengthening multisectoral and interdisciplinary institutional linkages and developing new alliances between ministries of agriculture and ministries of education as well as with civil society.

The educational needs of rural people have to remain a priority of international public organizations, donors, and in international deliberations and conferences. Specific focus on ERP is needed in the EFA Global Monitoring Report, and in declarations and recommendations of the next international conferences on poverty reduction and food security as well as on education, and at future EFA High-Level Group meetings.

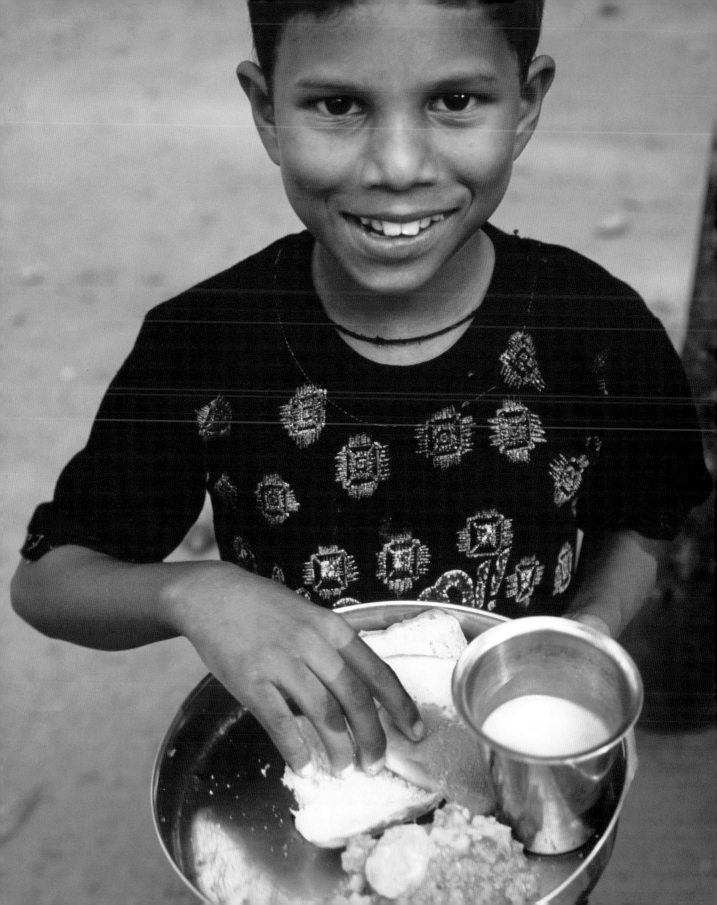

CONCLUSIONS and KEY POLICY CONSIDERATIONS

CONCLUSIONS AND KEY POLICY CONSIDERATIONS
REACHED IN THIS BOOK

>> **Progress to date.** Considerable progress has been made. Six years of policy, advocacy and capacity development work has led to important international recognition of ERP's key role in achieving the MDGs and especially of its key role in poverty alleviation, food security and sustainable natural resource management.

>> **More work remains.** Much work remains to be done. Despite the important progress made towards all eight MDGs, according to the United Nations, "we are not on track to fulfil our commitments" (UN, 2008 p. 3). There are many reasons for this, but lack of investment in education, training and capacity development of rural people is likely to be among the fundamental reasons for lack of progress.

>> **The value of ERP.** ERP is a public good and a long-term investment. Expanding and improving ERP is expensive but absolutely essential. There are strong arguments for investing in ERP. Better educated rural people have better employment prospects, better health, greater food security, less vulnerability to shocks, and better coping mechanisms in dealing with the forces of climate change, food crises, globalization and challenges to cultural traditions. Social stability, peace and democracy have a direct relation with inclusion of all citizens in education.

>> **ERP: a policy and programme priority.** Today's greater challenge for national governments, international agencies, bilateral donors and NGOs operating in education and training is to increase their policy and programme emphasis on ERP and ensure common monitoring of progress. The World Bank has increased its emphasis on agriculture and rural development. UNESCO, on the other hand, has de-emphasised the profile of "rural" in both its recent strategic plans and plans of work. UNESCO and the World Bank, given their lead roles in EFA and the Fast Track Initiative, can ensure that ERP becomes an integral part of Poverty Reduction

Strategy Papers and EFA National Plans. The EFA Fast Track Initiative can foster ERP by prioritizing support for those countries committed to promote education of their rural citizens.

>> **Financing ERP: a national and international priority.** UN Secretary-General indicates that "failure to provide Education for All puts an entire generation at risk" and that "right now, children from poor communities, rural areas and minority groups are almost always struggling to learn under worse conditions than others in society" (UN-DPI, 2008). As indicated by the Beijing EFA High-Level Group meeting, ERP needs to be a priority in national and international public resource allocations. ERP needs to be at the core of national plans for EFA and obtain an increased share of public funding. Capacity development initiatives to support long lasting resource allocation and implementation of these plans are needed. As stated in the foreword to *Education for rural development: towards new policy responses*, "business as usual" and "more of the same" will not permit these targets to be met either in rural areas or at a global level. Major policy and resource allocation shifts will need to take place if significant progress is to be made in EFA and poverty reduction.

>> **Reliable data on ERP.** Improved statistics as well as education management information systems are needed for effective policy planning, programme delivery, monitoring and evaluation of progress towards universal ERP and drawing lessons for better management and performance. Pro-poor policies call for disaggregated education and literacy data into rural and urban populations as is done for male and female populations in the UNESCO international statistics, the EFA Global Monitoring Report, as well as within national EMIS. Examples can be drawn from what is done for statistics of other development sectors.

>> **Partnerships.** Partnerships among international organizations, governments, non-governmental organizations, community-based organizations, universities and others will continue to be an essential ingredient of a successful ERP initiative.

>> **Intersectoral cooperation at national level.** At the national level, coordination between ministries of agriculture and education is essential if rural people are to be effectively served. Each of them has assets and expertise critical to these efforts, but neither has all the resources to pursue this alone. Coordination combined with capacity development for all professionals supporting ERP are important.

>> **Working as One UN: intersectoral cooperation at the international level.** As lead agency for the ERP partnership, FAO will continue to advocate for stronger governmental commitments for a higher level of resources for ERP. FAO, as a knowledge-based organization, will continue to collect, analyze, interpret and disseminate the knowledge required for the world to meet the food and nutrition needs of all its citizens and to provide global governance "with respect to ... the improvement of education and administration relating to nutrition, food and agriculture, and the spread of public knowledge of nutritional and agricultural science and practice" (FAO, 1945). FAO remains the only global resource for research, policy and technical expertise on agricultural education and training. The FAO Programme of Work and Budget focuses prevalently on technician training, literacy, skills training and lifelong learning for rural people, including extension as a means to support the transformation of agriculture. UNESCO and the World Bank are uniquely suited for facilitating ERP implementation at the national level, given that this role lies within their mandate to support the advancement of education that can be effectively pursued through their privileged dialogue with ministries of education. EFA National Plans, the Fast Track Initiative, poverty reduction strategies and national rural development plans as well as the One UN initiative can yield significant results as the lessons from the ERP first phase are implemented. UNESCO's leadership and technical support to ERP at the country level during this next phase would need to be strengthened, and FAO is in a good position to contribute as a supporting entity to the work of UNESCO in the specific areas of FAO expertise.

>> **Redefining agricultural education.** ERP will need to expand beyond the past approach whereby agricultural education for farmers was the primary focus of education in rural areas. Today, a broader view of the life and economic skills necessary to thrive in rural areas has emerged. There is a need to broaden the agricultural education paradigm to a paradigm of developing rural communities' capacity to promote sustainable rural development. Enhanced human capital in the rural space can be trained for increased on-farm productivity and for off-farm employment opportunities as well as learning that leads to improved social well-being, social capital formation and satisfactory livelihoods.

>> **Needs-based approach.** The "one size fits all" standardized education strategy is not effective in reaching rural people. At the national level, the hallmark of the ERP implementation will be a systemic needs-based approach. Mapping education and training (including extension) diversified needs of rural people and targeted interventions for expanding access and improving quality of education and training for all children, youth and adults through relevant curricula are crucial to success. Moreover, since the Paris Declaration in 2005, the idea has emerged that capacity development is largely an internally driven, endogenous process that can be stimulated but not directed from outside.

>> **Sharing policy lessons.** There are a number of policy alternatives to build rural people's capacity, self-esteem and resilience to address change and crises, many of which have been successfully implemented in various countries around the world. Dissemination of these lessons learned, best practices and research related to ERP is important to develop the capacity at national and regional levels to plan and implement effective policies. This book was designed to support capacity development initiatives such as the 2009 UNESCO World Conferences, and further activities, including ERP specific initiatives.

>> **Rural girls and women.** Rural girls and women suffer geographical and gender discrimination. Strategies to boost rural girls' participation in education and female literacy include removing cost barriers, strengthening rural schools as gender-sensitive centres of quality learning, developing gender-sensitive learning content and developing school and training centre facilities that take into account the needs of girls and women.

>> **Rural youth are the future.** Rural youth are the main protagonists for any future programme activity. Youth of today are the leaders and the farmers of tomorrow. Rural youth represent the majority of the population in the majority of less developed countries and explicit focus on their needs and contribution to our common future is urgent.

>> **ERP is a major challenge and an obvious opportunity.** The future challenges for ERP arise from the fact that the vast majority of those excluded from education live in rural areas. Therefore, ERP is vital, urgent and essential if the MDGs are to be met.

Final Communiqué of the Fifth Meeting of the High-Level Group on EFA
Maintaining the 2005 Beijing EFA High-Level Group Meeting recommendations on ERP

Education for rural people

"We, Heads of State, ministers, heads and top officials of multilateral and bilateral agencies, and leaders of non-governmental organizations, met in Beijing from 28 to 30 November 2005, at the invitation of the Director-General of UNESCO, for the Fifth Meeting of the High-Level Group on Education for All, whose central theme was literacy and education for rural people ....

12. Since the majority of those left behind and excluded from education live in rural areas, education for rural people is vital and urgent.

13. We recommend that Governments and EFA partners:

>> Invest more to reach and serve successfully the poorest, minorities, migrants, unorganised workers and other disadvantaged groups through best practices and other beneficial policies;

>> Design and implement targeted strategies, an intersectoral approach and strong partnerships to cater to the diversity of situations and needs;

>> In order to address the serious gap in the availability of teachers, design and urgently support strategies of teacher mobilisation and training programmes, including the UNESCO strategy for Teacher Training in sub-Saharan Africa. Where teachers remain insufficient in numbers, create alternative strategies and programmes.

>> Promote the quality of teaching and learning, with special attention to the strategies for placing, supporting and retaining qualified and trained teachers in rural areas and improving their working conditions;

>> Implement innovative measures, including curriculum reform, distance learning, non-formal education and application of ICTs, to improve relevance, respecting the diversity of local culture and languages, validating local knowledge and adopting flexible calendars; ..."

Source: Fifth Meeting of the High-Level Group on EFA 28–30 November 2005, Beijing, China. Final Communiqué

Photo credits

Alphabet letters (international glyphs) taken from:
Cimarosti, M. 2005. *Non legitur. Giro del mondo in trentatré scritture.* Stampa Alternativa e Graffiti.

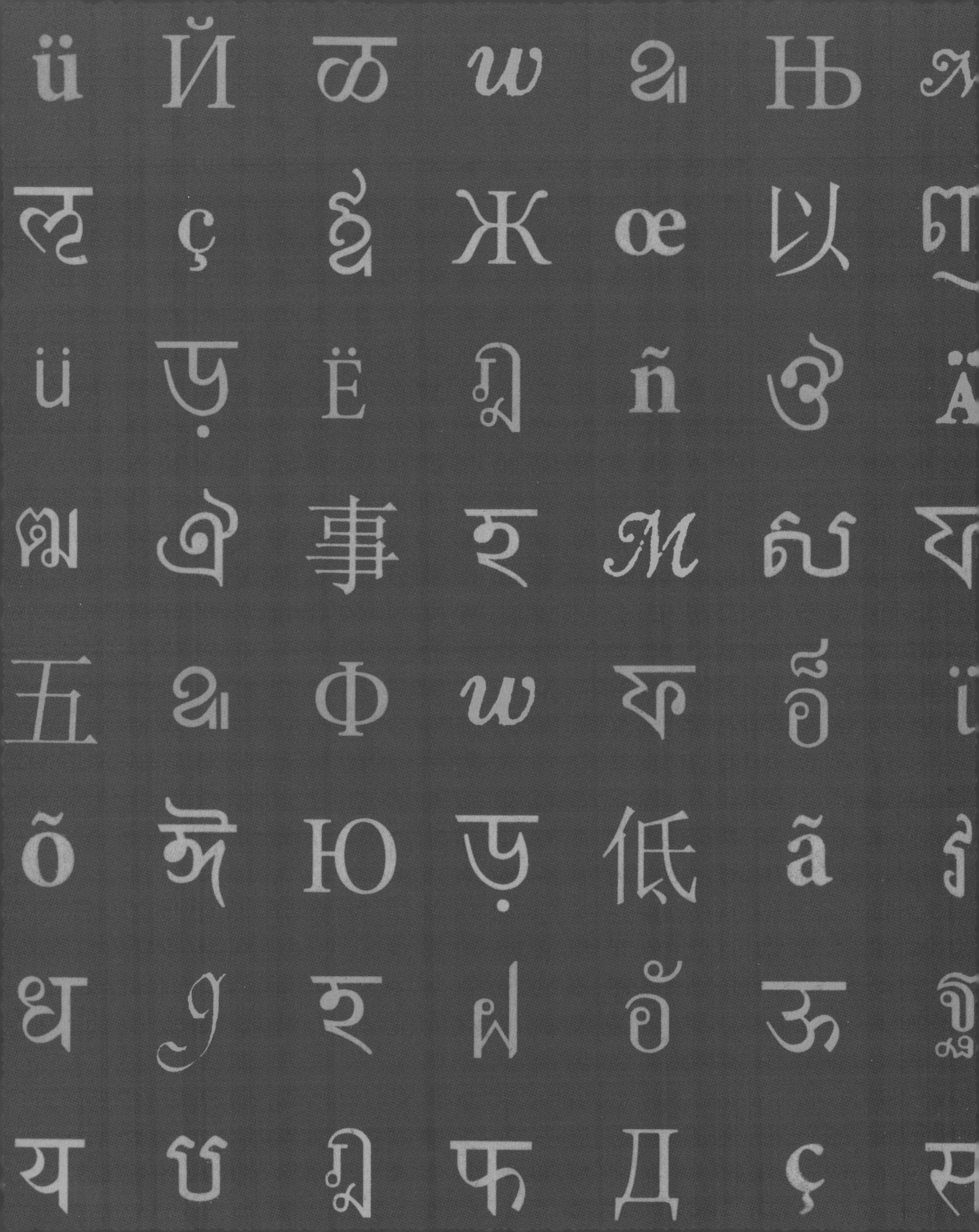

References

Acker, D. & Gasperini, L. 2003. Launching a new flagship on education for rural people: an initiative agricultural and extension educators can get behind. *Journal of International Agricultural and Extension Education,* 10(3): 81--85. Fall (also available at http://www.fao.org/sd/erp/ackerfall2003.pdf).

Acker, D. & Gasperini, L. 2008. Education for rural people: what have we learned. *Journal of International Agricultural and Extension Education,* 15(1). Spring (also available at http://www.fao.org/NR/edu/abst/edu_081001_en.htm).

ADB/UNESCO-IIEP. 2005. *The education of nomadic peoples in East Africa: Djibouti, Eritrea, Ethiopia, Kenya, Tanzania and Uganda,* by R. Carr-Hill & E. Peart. Tunis, African Development Bank and Paris, International Institute for Educational Planning (also available at unesdoc.unesco.org/images/0014/001405/140563e.pdf).

All Africa.com. 2007. *MDG – UN requires $110 billion to get children in school by 2015.* All Africa Global Media. 1 August (available at http://allafrica.com/stories/200707300343.html).

Anderlini, J. & Dyer, G. 2009. Downturn slashes 20m jobs in China. *Financial Times.* London, 3 February 2009, p. 1

Atchoarena, D. & Gasperini, L. 2003. in *Education for rural people: aid agencies workshop.* Rome, 12–13 December 2003. Rome, FAO and Paris, UNESCO (also available at ftp://ftp.fao.org/sd/SDR/SDRE/OxenhamRapportfinal.doc).

Avila, M., Atchoarena, D. & Gasperini, L. 2005a. *Agency approaches to skills development for rural people.* Paper presented to the Working Group for International Cooperation in Skills Development, November, Rome.

Avila, M., Atchoarena, D. & Gasperini, L. 2005b. Skills development for rural people: the FAO/ IIEP collaboration on education for rural people. In *Skills development for rural people: a renewed challenge.* pp. 14–19. Debates in Skills Management Paper 10. Geneva, Switzerland. Working Group for International Co-operation in Skills Development (also available at http://www.fao.org/sd/erp/Documents2006/Paper%2010.pdf).

Bunker, R. 2007. Ending poverty, but only on paper. *The American.* 30 July. (available at http://www.american.com/archive/2007/july-0707/ending-poverty-but-only-on-paper).

Burchi, F. & De Muro, P. 2007. *Education for rural people: a neglected key to food security?* Working paper No. 78. Rome, FAO and University of Roma Tre (also available at http://www.fao.org/sd/erp/ERPevents61_en.htm).

DFID (United Kingdom Department of International Development). 2007. Brown and Benn urge rich nations to boost aid to get all children into schools by 2015. *Press release.* 2 May. London (also available at http://www.dfid.gov.uk/news/files/pressreleases/children-into-school.asp).

Diouf, J. 2002. Speech at the launching of the new FAO/UNESCO Flagship Programme on Education for Rural People at the World Summit on Sustainable Development, 3 September. Johannesburg, South Africa (available at http://www.fao.org/sd/2002/kn0904_en.htm).

Diouf, J. 2009. Address to the High-Level Group Meeting on Food Security for All Madrid 26--27 January 2009 in his role as Director-General of the FAO and Vice-President of the UN High-Level Task Force on the Global Food Security Crisis (available at http://www.ransa2009.org/docs/docs/speech_DG_FAO_ransa2009.doc.pdf).

DOA (South African National Department of Agriculture)/FAO. 2003. *Agricultural education and training strategy for agriculture in rural development in South Africa.* (available at http://www.fao.org/sd/erp/documents2007/FinalStrategyNovember2003.pdf).

FAO. 1945. *The Constitution of FAO.* Article I. Rome (also available at http://www.fao.org/docrep/009/j8038e/j8038e00.htm).

FAO. 1997. *Higher agricultural education and opportunities in rural development for women. An overview and summary of five case studies,* by M. Karl. Rome (also available at http://www.fao.org/docrep/W6038E/W6038E00.htm).

FAO. 2000. *From agriculture education to education for rural development and food security: all for education and food for all*, by L. Gasperini. Paper presented at the Fifth European Conference on Higher Agricultural Education, 10–13 September. Plymouth, United Kingdom. SD Dimensions (available at http://www.fao.org/sd/EXdirect/EXre0028.htm).

FAO. 2002a. *Case study on education opportunities for hill tribes in Northern Thailand: implications for sustainable rural development,* by R. Fujioka. FAO RAP Publication 2002/05, Bangkok, Thailand (also available at ftp://ftp.fao.org/docrep/fao/004/AC383E/AC383E00.pdf).

FAO. 2002b. *Participatory curriculum development in agricultural education. A training guide,* by A. Rogers & P. Taylor. Rome (available at http://www.fao.org/sd/2002/KN0902_en.htm).

FAO. 2002c. *Targeting the rural poor: the role of education and training,* by L. Gasperini & C. Maguire. Paper presented at the International Working Group on Education, 10–21 November 2001, Lisbon, Portugal (available at http://www.fao.org/sd/2002/kn0301a_en.htm).

FAO. 2004a. *Educación para la población rural en Brasil, Chile, Colombia, Honduras, México, Paraguay y Perú.* FAO, UNESCO, DGCS Italia, CIDE, REDUC project. Rome (also available at http://www.fao.org/sd/erp/Estudio7paises.pdf).

FAO. 2004b. *Non-formal primary education for children of marine fisherfolk in Orissa, India,* by U. Tietze & N. Ray. Rome (also available at http://www.fao.org/docrep/007/ad822e/ad822e00.htm).

FAO. 2006. *The state of food insecurity in the world 2006.* Rome (also available at http://www.fao.org/docrep/009/a0750e/a0750e00.HTM).

FAO. 2007a. *Education and training for food security. Capacity building and good practices in five African countries.* Rome (also available at http://www.fao.org/sd/erp/documents2007/impaginatomaisOk.pdf).

FAO. 2007b. *Rural household access to assets and agrarian institutions: a cross country comparison,* by A. Zezza. ESA Working Paper No. 07-17, May. Agricultural Development Economic Division. Rome (available at ftp://ftp.fao.org/docrep/fao/010/ah854e/ah854e.pdf).

FAO. 2007c. *Education for rural people and food security. A cross-country analysis,* by F. Burchi & P. De Muro. Rome (also available at http://www.fao.org/docrep/010/a1434e/a1434e00.HTM).

FAO. 2008. *The state of food insecurity in the world 2008.* Rome (also available at http://www.fao.org/docrep/011/i0291e/i0291e00.htm).

FAO/ROMATRE. 2009. *Reducing children's food insecurity through primary education for rural mothers: the case of Mozambique,* by F. Burchi & P. De Muro. Rome, University of Roma Tre and FAO (available at http://www.fao.org/sd/erp/Documents2009/FAO-RomaTreFINALREPORT2.pdf).

FAO/UNESCO-IIEP. 2002. *Education for rural development in Asia: experiences and policy lessons,* by I. Birch, D. Atchoarena, L. Gasperini, H. Hakeem & M. Hazelman. Report of FAO/UNESCO Seminar 5–7 November 2002, Bangkok, Thailand. Paris, UNESCO (also available at ftp://ftp.fao.org/sd/SDR/SDRE/Mep_seminar_bangkok%20vFAO.PDF).

FAO/UNESCO-IIEP. 2003. *Education for rural development: towards new policy responses.* Coordinated and edited by D. Atchoarena & L. Gasperini. Rome, FAO and Paris, International Institute for Educational Planning, UNESCO (also in French Spanish and Chinese) (also available at ftp://ftp.fao.org/docrep/fao/006/ad423e/ad423e00.pdf; http://www.fao.org/sd/2003/KN12033_en.htm).

FAO/UNESCO-IIEP. 2004a. *Revisiting garden-based learning in basic education,* by D. Desmond, J. Grieshop & A. Subramanian. Rome, FAO and Paris, International Institute for Educational Planning, UNESCO (also available at http://www.fao.org/sd/erp/revisiting.pdf).

FAO/UNESCO-IIEP. 2004b. *The deep change process in Zamorano: 1997-2002,* by K.L. Andrews. Rome, FAO and Paris, International Institute for Educational Planning, UNESCO (also available at http://www.unesco.org/iiep).

FAO/UNESCO-IIEP. 2004c. *The reform of higher agricultural education institutions in China,* by L. Yonggong & Z. Jingzun. Rome, FAO and Paris, International Institute for Educational Planning (also available at http://www.fao.org/sd/erp/documents2007/china.pdf).

FAO/UNESCO-IIEP. 2005a. *Education for rural people to achieve EFA and the MGDs,* by L. Gasperini & D. Atchoarena. Background paper to the Sixth Meeting of the Working Group on EFA, 19–21 July 2005, UNESCO, Paris. (also available at http://www.fao.org/sd/erp/documents2005/ WGEFA background.pdf).

FAO/UNESCO-IIEP. 2005b. *Seminario "Educación para la población rural (EPR) en América Latina". Alimentación y educación para todos.* Santiago, Chile, 3–5 August 2004. Rome, FAO and Paris, International Institute for Educational Planning, UNESCO (also available at http://www.fao.org/sd/erp/documents2007/MEPFAO_A_Latina.pdf).

FAO/UNESCO-IIEP. 2005c. *Reforming higher agricultural education institutions. The case of the School of Agriculture at Monterrey Tech (ITESM),* by M. Zertuche. Rome, FAO and Paris, International Institute for Educational Planning, UNESCO (also available at ftp://ftp.fao. org/docrep/fao/010/ai222e/ai222e.pdf).

FAO/UNESCO-IIEP. 2005d. *Higher education for rural development: the experience of the University of Cordoba,* by E. Ramos & M. del Mar Delgado. Rome, FAO and Paris, International Institute for Educational Planning, UNESCO (also available at www.fao.org/SD/ERP/documents2007/ MEPFAO_Spain_Cordoba.pdf).

FAO/UNESCO-IIEP. 2006a. *Addressing learning needs of rural people in Asia,* by C. Haddad. Series coordinated and edited by D. Atchoarena & L. Gasperini, Rome, FAO and Paris, International Institute for Educational Planning, UNESCO (also available at http://www.fao.org/sd/erp/ documents2007/Mep_Bangkok%20report.pdf).

FAO/UNESCO-IIEP. 2006b. *Education for rural people in Africa.* Rome, FAO and Paris, International Institute for Educational Planning, UNESCO (available at http://www.fao.org/sd/erp/ documents2007/Mep_Addisseminarsecured.pdf).

FAO/UNESCO-IIEP. 2006c. *Caribbean Conference on Education for Rural People: food security, agricultural competitiveness, sustainable livelihoods.* 18–19 May 2006. St. Lucia (available at http://www.fao.org/sd/erp/ERPevents48_en.htm).

FAO/UNESCO-IIEP. 2007a. *Seminar on higher education and international co-operation: role and strategies for universities.* 27–29 September 2006. Agropolis, Montpellier (available at http://www.fao.org/sd/erp/ERPevents51_en.htm).

FAO/UNESCO-IIEP. 2007b. *Using indicators in planning education for rural people: a practical guide,* by C. Sauvageot & P. Da Graça. Rome, FAO and Paris, International Institute for Educational Planning, UNESCO (also available at http://www.fao.org/sd/erp/documents2007/ Indicators_guide.pdf).

FAO/World Bank. 2000. *Agriculture knowledge and information systems for rural development (AKIS/RD): strategic vision and guiding principles.* Rome, FAO and World Bank (also available at ftp://ftp.fao.org/SD/SDR/SDRE/AKIS.pdf).

Gasperini, L. 2001. *World Food Summit five years on: the challenge of feeding and educating all.* Paper presented at the Global Consortium of Higher Education and Research for Agriculture and Food Systems in the 21st Century, San Francisco, 14 July (also available at http://www.gchera.iastate.edu/conf2001/ and in SD Dimension, FAO http://www.fao.org/sd/2001/kn1005a_en.htm).

Government of South Africa/FAO. 2003. National strategy on education and training for agriculture and rural development in South Africa (also available at http://www.fao.org/sd/erp/documents2007/terminalstatementSA1.pdf).

Greenway, H.D.S. 2009. Moving back from the coast. *International Herald Tribune*, 28 January (available at http://www.iht.com/articles/2009/01/28/opinion/edgreenway.php).

IFAD. 2001. *Rural poverty report: the challenge of ending rural poverty.* Rome, International Fund for Agricultural Development (also available at http://www.ifad.org/poverty/index.htm).

IFPRI. 2004. *Impact of feeding children in school: evidence from Bangladesh.* Washington, DC. International Food Policy Research Institute (available at http://documents.wfp.org/stellent/groups/public/documents/liaison_offices/wfp121947.pdf).

LaFraniere, S. 2009. 20 million migrants in China can't find work. *International Herald Tribune.* 3 February 2009.

MEST/MAFRD/FAO. 2004. *A strategy for education for rural people in Kosovo.* Ministry of Education, Science and Technology and Ministry of Agriculture, Forestry and Rural Development of Kosovo, Pristina, FAO (also available at http://www.fao.org/sd/erp/ERPkosovoenglish.PDF).

Moock, P.R. 1981. Education and technical efficiency in small-farm production. *Economic Development and Cultural Change,* 29(4): 723-739, University of Chicago Press, United States of America.

Psacharopoulos, G. 1994. Returns to investment in education: a global update. *World Development,* 22(9):1325-43, Amsterdam, Elsevier.

SIDA. 2000. *Capacity development as a strategic question in development cooperation.* Capacity Development - Sida Working Paper No. 8. Stockholm, Swedish International Development Assistance (also available at www.sida.se/shared/jsp/download.jsp?f=Wp8.pdf&a=2474).

UN Millennium Project. 2005. *Toward universal primary education: investments, incentives, and institutions.* Task Force on Education and Gender Equality. London, EARTHSCAN (also available at http://www.unmillenniumproject.org/documents/Education-complete.pdf).

UN. 2002. FAO and UNESCO propose a joint partnership to promote education in the rural world. UN System Network on Rural Development and Food Security (available at http://www.rdfs.net/news/news/0210ne/0210ne_FAOUNESCO_en.htm).

UN. 2004. *Report of the Secretary-General on the work of the Organization*. General Assembly Official Records, Fifty-ninth Session, Supplement No. 1 (A/59/1), New York (also available at http://daccess-ods.un.org/TMP/910693.9.html).

UN. 2008. *The Millennium Development Goals Report 2008*. New York, United Nations, Department of Economic and Social Affairs (also available at http://www.undp.org/publications/MDG_Report_2008_En.pdf).

UN-DESA. 2008. *World urbanization prospects: the 2007 revision. Highlights*. New York, United Nations, Department of Economic and Social Affairs/ Population Division. (also available at http://www.un.org/esa/population/publications/wup2007/2007WUP_Highlights_web.pdf).

UNDP. 1999. *Human Development Report 1999*. New York, Oxford University Press (also available at http://hdr.undp.org/en/media/HDR_1999_EN.pdf).

UN-DPI. 2008. *Secretary-General, in message, says education can drive economic, social progress. Failure to provide education for all puts entire generation at risk*. United Nations Secretary-General Message (SG/SM/11819), 25 September. New York, United Nations, Department of Public Information (also available at: http://www.un.org/News/Press/docs//2008/sgsm11819.doc.htm).

UNESCO. 2000. *The Dakar framework for action*. Adopted by the World Education Forum, Dakar, Senegal, 26-28 April 2000. Paris, UNESCO (also available at unesdoc.unesco.org/images/0012/001211/121147E.pdf).

UNESCO. 2005. *Fifth Meeting of the High-Level Group on Education for All*. 28–30 November. Beijing, China. Final Communiqué, Paris (also available at http://www.fao.org/sd/erp/beijingdocuments/EFA%20HLG%202005%20Communique%20Final.doc).

UNESCO. 2007. *EFA Global Monitoring Report 2008*. Paris, Oxford University Press (also available at http://www.unesco.org/en/education/efareport/reports/2008-mid-term-review/).

UNESCO. 2008. *EFA Global Monitoring Report 2009*. Paris, Oxford University Press (also available at http://www.unesco.org/en/education/efareport/reports/2009-governance/).

UNESCO-IIEP. 2003. *Les classes multigrades: une contribution au développement de la scolarisation en milieu rural africain?* by E. Brunswic & J. Valérien. Paris, International Institute for Educational Planning, UNESCO (also available at unesdoc.unesco.org/images/0013/001362/136280f.pdf).

UNESCO-IIEP. 2007. *Advancing in education: reaching rural people, developing capacities*. Report from the IWGE Meeting in Rome, Italy, 12–14 June 2006. Paris, UNESCO-IIEP International Working Group on Education. (also available at unesdoc.unesco.org/images/0015/001538/153896e.pdf).

UNESCO-UIS. 2005. *Children out of school: measuring exclusion from primary education*. Montreal, Canada, UNESCO Institute of Statistics (also available at http://www.uis.unesco.org/template/pdf/educgeneral/OOSC_EN_WEB_FINAL.pdf).

UNICEF. 1992. *The case for investing in basic education*. New York, UNICEF.

Van Crowder, L., Lindley, W.I., Bruening, T.H. & Doron, N. 1998. Agricultural education for sustainable rural development: challenges for developing countries in the 21st century. *Journal of Agricultural Education and Extension,*. 5(2): 71–84, New York, USA, Routledge (available at http://www.fao.org/sd/Exdirect/Exan0025.htm).

Working Group for International Cooperation in Skills Development. 2005. *Skills development for rural people: a renewed challenge*. Paper No. 10, Geneva, Switzerland (also available at http://www.fao.org/sd/erp/Documents2006/Paper%2010.pdf).

World Bank. 1988. Education and development: a review, by G. Psacharopoulos. *The World Bank Research Observer* 3 (1): 99-116. (available at: http://wbro.oxfordjournals.org/cgi/content/abstract/3/1/99).

World Bank. 2007a. *Cultivating knowledge and skills to grow African agriculture. A synthesis of an institutional, regional, and international review*. Report No. 40997-AFR. Washington, DC, World Bank, International Bank for Reconstruction and Development (also available at http://siteresources.worldbank.org/INTARD/Resources/AET_Final_web.pdf).

World Bank. 2007b. *New evidence on the urbanization of global poverty,* by M. Ravaillion, S. Chen & P. Sangraula. Policy Research Working Paper 4199, April. Washington, DC (also available at http://siteresources.worldbank.org/INTWDR2008/Resources/2795087-1191427986785/RavallionMEtAl_UrbanizationOfGlobalPoverty.pdf).

World Bank. 2007c. *World Development Report 2008: agriculture for development*. New York, Oxford University Press. IBDR/World Bank (also available at: www.worldbank.org/wdr2008*)*.

Selected publications on ERP
The ERP website can be found at www.fao.org/sd/erp

Books
Available at http://www.fao.org/sd/erp/ERPpublications_en.htm

ADB/UNESCO-IIEP. 2005. *The education of nomadic peoples in East Africa: Djibouti, Eritrea, Ethiopia, Kenya, Tanzania and Uganda,* by R. Carr-Hill & E. Peart. Tunis, African Development Bank and Paris, International Institute for Educational Planning (also available at unesdoc. unesco.org/images/0014/001405/140563e.pdf).

Burchi, F. & De Muro, P. 2007. *Education for rural people: a neglected key to food security?* Working Paper No. 78. Rome, FAO and University of Roma Tre (also available at http://www. fao.org/sd/erp/ERPevents61_en.htm).

CGIAR. 2006. *Evaluation and impact of training in the CGIAR.* Science Council of the Consultative Group on International Agricultural Research (also available at documents2009/Evaluation_ and_Impact_of_Training.pdf).

DgCiD. 2008. *Systèmes de production, revenus et pratiques de scolarisation des agriculteurs: études de cas dans trois régions du Sénégal.* Montpellier, France. Ministère des Affaires étrangères et européennes, Direction générale de la Coopération internationale et du développement (also available at documents2009/687_scolar_agriculteurs.pdf).

FAO. 1990. *Make learning easier. A guide for improving educational/training materials.* Rome (also available at www.fao.org/sd/erp/ERPPublications_en.htm).

FAO. 1991. *Improving training quality. A trainer's guide to evaluation.* Rome (also available at ftp://ftp.fao.org/docrep/fao/010/ai230e/ai230e.pdf).

FAO. 1994. *Ecología y enseñanza rural 121.* Rome, FAO Forestry Division (also available at http:// www.fao.org/DOCREP/006/T3725S/t3725s00.htm).

FAO. 1996. *Ecología y enseñanza rural 131.* Rome FAO Forestry Division (also available at http:// www.fao.org/DOCREP/006/W1309S/W1309S00.HTM).

FAO. 2001. *Distance education and distance learning: a framework for the Food and Agriculture Organization of the United Nations,* by S. Mclean. Rome (available at http://www.fao.org/ sd/2001/KN0901a_en.htm).

FAO. 2001. *Participatory environment education and training for sustainable agriculture. Best practices in institutional partnership, peer learning and networking.* Rome (also available at http://www.fao.org/DOCREP/006/Y0923E/y0923e00.htm).

FAO. 2002. *Case study on education opportunities for hill tribes in Northern Thailand: implications for sustainable rural development,* by R. Fujioka. FAO RAP Publication 2002/05, Bangkok, Thailand (also available at ftp://ftp.fao.org/docrep/fao/004/AC383E/AC383E00.pdf).

FAO. 2002. *Participatory curriculum development in agricultural education. A training guide,* by A. Rogers & P. Taylor. Rome (available at http://www.fao.org/sd/2002/KN0902_en.htm).

FAO. 2004. *Educación para la población rural en Brasil, Chile, Colombia, Honduras, México, Paraguay y Perú.* FAO, UNESCO, DGCS Italia, CIDE, REDUC project. Rome, FAO (also available at http://www.fao.org/sd/erp/Estudio7paises.pdf).

FAO. 2004. *The state of food insecurity in the world 2004.* Rome (also available at www.fao.org/docrep/007/y5650e/y5650e00.htm).

FAO. 2005. *The state of food insecurity in the world 2005.* Rome (also available at http://www.fao.org/docrep/008/a0200e/a0200e00.htm).

FAO. 2007. *Education and training for food security. Capacity building and good practices in five African countries.* Rome (also available at http://www.fao.org/sd/erp/documents2007/impaginatomaisOk.pdf).

FAO. 2007. *Education for rural people and food security. A cross-country analysis,* by F. Burchi & P. De Muro. Rome (also available at http://www.fao.org/docrep/010/a1434e/a1434e00.HTM).

FAO/APEAEN. 2003. *Best practices for education and training of rural youth - Lesson from Asia.* Bangkok, Thailand. FAO Regional Office ad Asia Pacific Association of Educators in Agriculture and Environment (also available at http://www.fao.org/sd/erp/ERPpublications_en.htm).

FAO/APEAEN. 2008. *Preparing for the future: rethinking higher agriculture education and environment in the Asia Pacific.* Third International Conference on Agriculture Education and Environment, FAO and Asia Pacific Association of Educators in Agriculture Education and Environment (also available at http://www.fao.org/sd/erp/RethinkingHigherEducation_en.htm).

FAO/UNESCO-IIEP. 2002. *Education for rural development in Asia: experiences and policy lessons,* by I. Birch, D. Atchoarena, L. Gasperini, H. Hakeem & M. Hazelman. Report of FAO/UNESCO Seminar, 5–7 November 2002, Bangkok, Thailand. Paris, UNESCO (also available at ftp://ftp.fao.org/sd/SDR/SDRE/Mep_seminar_bangkok%20vFAO.PDF).

FAO/UNESCO-IIEP. 2003. *Education for rural development: towards new policy responses.* Coordinated and edited by D. Atchoarena & L. Gasperini. Rome, FAO and Paris, International Institute for Educational Planning, UNESCO (also in French, Spanish and Chinese) (also available at ftp://ftp.fao.org/docrep/fao/006/ad423e/ad423e00.pdf; http://www.fao.org/sd/2003/KN12033_en.htm).

FAO/UNESCO-IIEP. 2003. *Education for rural people: aid agencies workshop.* Rome, FAO and Paris, International Institute for Educational Planning, UNESCO (also available at http://www.fao.org/sd/2003/KN0604_en.htm).

FAO/UNESCO-IIEP. 2004. *Revisiting garden-based learning in basic education,* by D. Desmond, J. Grieshop & A. Subramaniam. Rome, FAO and Paris, International Institute for Educational Planning, UNESCO (also available at http://www.fao.org/sd/erp/revisiting.pdf).

FAO/UNESCO-IIEP. 2004. *The deep change process in Zamorano: 1997-2002,* by K.L. Andrews. Rome, FAO and Paris, International Institute for Educational Planning, UNESCO (also available at http://www.unesco.org/iiep).

FAO/UNESCO-IIEP. 2004. *The reform of higher agricultural education institutions in China,* by L. Yonggong & Z. Jingzun. Rome, FAO and Paris, International Institute for Educational Planning (also available at http://www.fao.org/sd/erp/documents2007/china.pdf).

FAO/UNESCO-IIEP. 2004. *Training for rural development in Brazil: SENAR,* by C.A. Gomes & J. Câmara. Rome, FAO and Paris, International Institute for Educational Planning, UNESCO (also available at www.fao.org/SD/ERP/fao_brazil.pdf).

FAO/UNESCO-IIEP. 2005. *Higher education for rural development: the experience of the University of Cordoba,* by E. Ramos & M. del Mar Delgado. Rome, FAO and Paris, International Institute for Educational Planning, UNESCO (also available at www.fao.org/SD/ERP/documents2007/MEPFAO_Spain_Cordoba.pdf).

FAO/UNESCO-IIEP. 2005. *Reforming higher agricultural education institutions. The case of the School of Agriculture at Monterrey Tech (ITESM),* by M. Zertuche. Rome, FAO and Paris, International Institute for Educational Planning, UNESCO (also available at ftp://ftp.fao.org/docrep/fao/010/ai222e/ai222e.pdf).

FAO/UNESCO-IIEP. 2005. *Seminario "Educación para la población rural (EPR) en América Latina".* *Alimentación y educación para todos.* Santiago de Chile, 3–5 August 2004. Rome, FAO and Paris, International Institute for Educational Planning, UNESCO (also available at http://www.fao.org/sd/erp/documents2007/MEPFAO_A_Latina.pdf).

FAO/UNESCO-IIEP. 2006. *Addressing learning needs of rural people in Asia,* by C. Haddad. Series coordinated and edited by D. Atchoarena & L. Gasperini. Rome, FAO and Paris, International Institute for Educational Planning, UNESCO (also available at http://www.fao.org/sd/erp/documents2007/Mep_Bangkok%20report.pdf).

FAO/UNESCO-IIEP. 2006. *Caribbean Conference on Education for Rural People: food security, agricultural competitiveness, sustainable livelihoods.* 18–19 May 2006, St. Lucia (available at http://www.fao.org/sd/erp/ERPevents48_en.htm).

FAO/UNESCO-IIEP. 2006. *Education for rural people in Africa.* Rome, FAO and Paris, International Institute for Educational Planning, UNESCO (available at http://www.fao.org/sd/erp/documents2007/Mep_Addisseminarsecured.pdf).

FAO/UNESCO-IIEP. 2007. *Using indicators in planning education for rural people: a practical guide,* by C. Sauvageot & P. Da Graça. Rome, FAO and Paris, International Institute for Educational Planning, UNESCO (also available at http://www.fao.org/sd/erp/documents2007/Indicators_guide.pdf).

Gasperini, L. 2003. Education for rural people: a crucial factor for sustainable development. FAO Journal *Food, Nutrition and Agriculture* no. 33. Rome (available at ftp://ftp.fao.org/docrep/fao/006/j0243m/j0243m02.pdf).

Gasperini, L. 2003. Education for rural people: addressing a neglected majority. *Commonwealth Education Partnerships 2003* (available at http://www.fao.org/sd/ERP/documents2008/27EDFORR.pdf)

Government of South Africa/FAO. 2003. National strategy on education and training for agriculture and rural development in South Africa. (also available at http://www.fao.org/sd/erp/documents2007/terminalstatementSA1.pdf)   (http://www.fao.org/sd/erp/RethinkingHigherEducation_en.htm).

MEST/MAFRD/FAO. 2004. *A strategy for education for rural people in Kosovo*. Ministry of Education, Science and Technology and Ministry of Agriculture, Forestry and Rural Development of Kosovo, Pristina, FAO (also available at http://www.fao.org/sd/erp/ERPkosovoenglish.PDF).

UNESCO. 2004. *EFA flagships initiatives. Multi-partner collaborative mechanisms in support of EFA goals*. Paris (also available at unesdoc.unesco.org/images/0013/001356/135639e.pdf).

UNESCO. Education today. (available at http://portal.unesco.org/education)

UNESCO-IIEP. 2003. *Les classes multigrades: une contribution au développement de la scolarisation en milieu rural africain?* by E. Brunswic & J. Valérien. Paris, International Institute for Educational Planning, UNESCO (also available at unesdoc.unesco.org/images/0013/001362/136280f.pdf).

UNESCO-IIEP. 2007. *Advancing in education: reaching rural people, developing capacities*. Report from the IWGE Meeting in Rome, Italy, 12–14 June 2006. Paris, UNESCO-IIEP International Working Group on Education. (also available at unesdoc.unesco.org/images/0015/001538/153896e.pdf).

Working Group for International Cooperation in Skills Development. 2005. *Skills development for rural people: a renewed challenge*. Paper No. 10, Geneva, Switzerland (also available at http://www.fao.org/sd/erp/Documents2006/Paper%2010.pdf).

World Bank. 2007. *Cultivating knowledge and skills to grow African agriculture. A synthesis of an institutional, regional, and international review*. Report No. 40997-AFR. Washington, DC, World Bank, International Bank for Reconstruction and Development (also available at http://siteresources.worldbank.org/INTARD/Resources/AET_Final_web.pdf).

Virtual publications
Available at http://www.fao.org/sd/erp/ERPvirtualpublications_en.htm

Announcement of the Aid Agencies Workshop on *Education for Rural People: targeting the poor*, Rome, Italy, 12–-13 December 2002. FAO SD Dimensions, December 2002 (available at http://www.fao.org/sd/2002/KN1202_en.htm).

Atchoarena, D. & Gasperini, L. 2005. *Education for rural people (ERP) to achieve EFA and the MDGs.* FAO and UNESCO Back Ground Paper (available at http://www.fao.org/sd/erp/documents2005/WGEFA%20background.pdf).

Atchoarena, D. 2006. *The contribution of higher education to learning and development in rural areas: experiences and policy implications.* UNESCO-IIEP Working Document (available at http://www.unesco.org/iiep/eng/networks/iwge/2006/I_5a.pdf).

Atchoarena, D. & Holmes, K. 2005. The role of agricultural colleges and universities in rural development and lifelong learning in Asia. *Asian Journal of Agriculture and Development*, 2 (1-2): 15–24 (available at http://www.fao.org/sd/erp/Documents2007/atchoarenakeithholmes.pdf).

Avila, M. & Gasperini, L. 2005. *The MDGs and sustainable rural development in Sub-Saharan Africa. Challenges and implications for Education for Rural People (ERP)* FAO SD Dimensions, November 2005 (available at http://www.fao.org/sd/dim_kn2/kn2_051101_en.htm).

Baronio, S. 2005. Le projet « Education pour tous » dans un contexte rural au Sénégal (available at http://www.fao.org/sd/erp/Documents2007/leprojetEPT.pdf).

Bergmann, H. 2003. *Practical subjects in basic education. Relevance at last or second rate education? Lessons from 40 years of experience.* FAO SD Dimensions, April (available at http://www.fao.org/sd/2003/KN0402_en.htm).

Brochure on Education for Rural People printed for the *People Centred Development Day* (available at http://www.unesco.org/education/efa/know_sharing/flagship_initiatives/rural_education.pdf).

Diouf, J. 2002. Speech at the launching of the new FAO/UNESCO Flagship Programme on Education for Rural People at the World Summit on Sustainable Development, 3 September, Johannesburg, South Africa (available at http://www.fao.org/sd/2002/kn0904_en.htm).

Education opportunities for hill tribes in Northern Thailand: implications for sustainable rural development. FAO SD Dimensions, July 2002 (available at http://www.fao.org/sd/2002/kn0704_en.htm).

Eicher, C.K. 2006. *The evolution of agricultural education and training: global insights of relevance for Africa.* Michigan State University, August (available at http://www.fao.org/sd/erp/Documents2006/globalAETInsightsEicher.pdf).

Emiliani, M. & Gasperini, L. 2002. *Compendium of experiences of Italian NGOs in education for rural people.* FAO SD Dimensions, October (available at http://www.fao.org/sd/2002/KN1002_en.htm).

ERP Coordination Unit. 2005. *French NGOs and the FAO/UNESCO Programme Education for Rural People.* FAO SD Dimensions, June (available in French at http://www.fao.org/sd/dim_kn2/kn2_050602_en.htm).

FAO and UNESCO propose a Joint Partnership to promote education in the rural world. UN System Network on Rural Development and Food Security, October 2002 (available at http://www.rdfs.net/news/news/0210ne/0210ne_FAOUNESCO_en.htm).

FAO, Government of Chile, Chilean University & Institute of Nutrition and Food Technology. *Educación en alimentación y nutrición para la enseñanza basica* (Spanish) (available at http://www.rlc.fao.org/prior/segalim/accalim/educa.htm and http://www.rlc.fao.org/prior/segalim/accalim/educa/default.htm).

Feldberg, K.B. 2007. *Some reflections on rural education with Norway as a case.*

Centre for International Education, Oslo University College. March (available at http://www.fao.org/sd/erp/Documents2007/RuraleducationinNorway.doc).

Final Communiqué on the Aid Agencies Workshop on *Education for Rural People: targeting the poor.* Rome, 12–13 December 2002. FAO SD Dimensions, January 2003 (available at http://www.fao.org/sd/2003/KN0102a_en.htm).

Final Communiqué on workshop on *Education for Rural Development in Asia: experiences and policy lessons.* Bangkok, Thailand, 5–7 November 2002. FAO SD Dimensions, December 2002 (available at http://www.fao.org/sd/2002/KN1201_en.htm).

Gasperini, L. & Maguire, C. 2002. *Targeting the rural poor: the role of education and training.* FAO SD Dimensions, March (available at http://www.fao.org/sd/2002/kn0301a_en.htm).

Gasperini, L. & McLean, S. 2001. *Education for agriculture and rural development in low-income countries: implications of the digital divide.* FAO SD Dimensions, March (available at http://www.fao.org/sd/2001/kn0301a_en.htm).

Gasperini, L. 2000. *From agricultural education to education for rural development and food security: all for education and food for all.* FAO SD Dimensions, October (available at http://www.fao.org/sd/exdirect/exre0028.htm).

Gasperini, L. 2001. *World Food Summit five years later: the challenge of feeding and educating all.* FAO SD Dimensions, October (available at http://www.fao.org/sd/2001/kn1005a_en.htm).

Gasperini, L. 2003. Education for rural people, a crucial factor for sustainable development. FAO journal *Food, Nutrition and Agriculture*, No. 33 (available at ftp://ftp.fao.org/docrep/fao/006/j0243m/j0243m02.pdf).

Gasperini, L. 2003. Education for rural people: addressing a neglected majority *Commonwealth Education Partnership 2003* (available at http://www.15ccem.com/15CCEM/files/CEP2003/27EDFORR.PDF).

Gautier, P. & Eberlin, R. 2003. *Education for rural people as a component of a rural development strategy for Croatia*. FAO SD Dimensions, October (available at http://www.fao.org/sd/2003/kn10043_en.htm).

Hermanowicz, E. 2007. *Education for rural people. Main policy issues.* (available at http://www.fao.org/sd/erp/Documents2007/ThesisonERPMainPolicyIssue.pdf).

International Bank for Reconstruction and Development/World Bank. 2007 *Cultivating knowledge and skills to grow African agriculture. A synthesis of an institutional, regional, and international review* (available at http://www.nasulgc.org/NetCommunity/Document.Doc?id=1189).

Maguire, C. 2001. *From agriculture to rural development: critical choices for agriculture education.* FAO SD Dimensions, April (available at http://www.fao.org/sd/2001/kn0401_en.htm).

McLean, S., Gasperini, L. & Rudgard, S. 2002. Distance learning for food security and rural development: a perspective from the United Nations Food and Agriculture Organization. *The International Review of Research in Open and Distance Learning (IRRODLT).* April (available at http://www.irrodl.org/content/v3.1/mclean.html).

Mingat, A. 2004. *Magnitude of social disparities in primary education in Africa: gender, geographical location, and family income in the context of Education for All (EFA).* FAO SD Dimensions, October (available at http://www.fao.org/sd/dim_kn2/kn2_041001_en.htm).

Muehlhoff, E. 2005. Can nutrition education make a difference? *International Congress on Nutrition.* Durban, South Africa, 19–23 September (available at ftp://ftp.fao.org/ag/agn/nutrition/muehlhoff_fao.pdf).

Riedmiller, S. 2002. *Primary school agriculture: what can it realistically achieve?* FAO SD Dimensions, July (available at http://www.fao.org/sd/2002/kn0701_en.htm).

Rogers, A., Taylor, P., Lindley, W.I., Van Crowder, L. & Soddemann, M. 2002. *Participatory curriculum development study: a training guide.* FAO SD Dimensions, September (also available at http://www.fao.org/sd/2002/KN0902_en.htm).

Sommer, K.N., Sorflate, L. & Lortie, J. A. 2001. *Compendium of FAO experience in basic education: all for education and food for all.* FAO SD Dimensions, October (available at http://www.fao.org/sd/2001/kn1003_en.htm).

Temu, A.B., Rudebjer, P.G., Kiyiapi, J. & Van Lierop, P. 2005. Forestry education in Sub-Saharan Africa and Southeast Asia: trends, myths and realities. Rome (available at http://www.fao.org/docrep/008/j4605e/j4605e00.htm).

Valentini, A. *Malawi's rural adolescent girls education.* FAO Sustainable Development Department (available at http://www.fao.org/sd/erp/malawi.pdf).

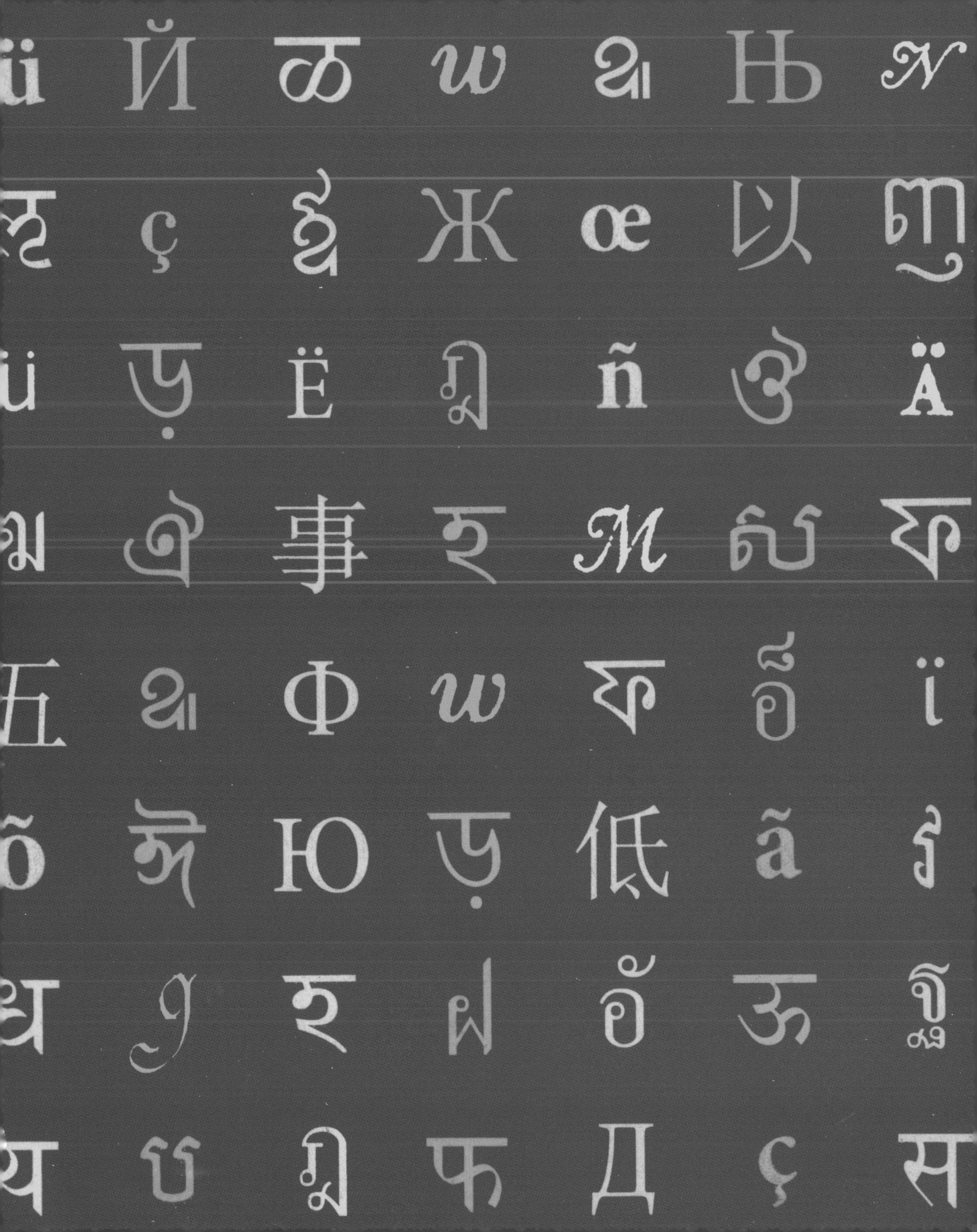

Printed in Italy on ecological paper, May 2009